12/24/07

P9-BZO-630

Dear Kimmie -

I really believe there
is no more powerful thing
in the world than
sincere prayer -

I love you
Karen

HOW
STRONG
WOMEN
PRAY

HOW
STRONG
WOMEN
PRAY

Bonnie St. John

Faith
Words ®

NEW YORK   BOSTON   NASHVILLE

Scriptures noted KJV are taken from the King James Version of the Bible.

Scriptures noted NIV are taken from the HOLY BIBLE: NEW INTERNATIONAL VERSION®. Copyright © 1973, 1978, 1984 by International Bible Society. Used by permission of Zondervan Publishing House. All rights reserved.

Scriptures noted NKJV are taken from the NEW KING JAMES VERSION. Copyright © 1979, 1980, 1982, Thomas Nelson, Inc., Publishers.

Scriptures noted NRSV are taken from the NEW REVISED STANDARD VERSION of the Bible. Copyright © 1989 by the Division of Christian Education of the National Council of The Churches of Christ in the U.S.A. All rights reserved.

FaithWords
Hachette Book Group USA
237 Park Avenue
New York, NY 10017

Visit our Web site at www.faithwords.com.

Printed in the United States of America

First Edition: November 2007

10 9 8 7 6 5 4 3 2 1

FaithWords® is a division of Hachette Book Group USA, Inc.
The FaithWords name and logo is a trademark of Hachette Book Group USA, Inc.

Library of Congress Cataloging-in-Publication Data

St. John, Bonnie.
   How strong women pray / Bonnie St. John.—1st ed.
      p. cm.
   Summary: "Bonnie St. John profiles some of today's most prominent women and how prayer has impacted their lives."—Provided by the publisher.
   ISBN-13: 978-0-446-57926-1
   ISBN-10: 0-446-57926-2
   1. Women—Religious life.   2. Prayer—Christianity.   I. Title.
   BV4527.S723 2007
   248.3'2082—dc22

                                                        2007014147

DEDICATED TO THE MEMORY OF MY MOTHER

RUBY C. SCHWIMMER

DECEMBER 27, 1939—DECEMBER 30, 2006

A strong woman whose prayers made this book possible.

CONTENTS

CONTENTS

INTRODUCTION

People ask me how I got the idea for *How Strong Women Pray*. Actually, I was praying.

I was sitting on my living-room floor in New York City praying one morning several years ago, as was my routine at the time. I had come to a point in my life where I looked forward to these moments I shared with God at the start of every day. Not because anything was particularly wrong. So often, prayer is relegated to moments of dire need. No, praying for me had become a source of well-being, joy, and faith. As I prayed, I would feel physically strengthened—from good to better than good. I remember appreciating how much I had drawn from prayer over the years. Feeling uplifted in the good times and, in bad times, finding the courage to move forward. I knew that learning how to pray was one of the most important things I had ever done.

Without prayer, I would have collapsed under the weight of the difficulties in my life and failed as a mother. I would not have been able to inspire others to overcome their own obstacles. I am not sure who I would be at all.

Yet, most people who knew me as a strong woman—an inspirational speaker, a one-legged Olympic ski champion, a Rhodes Scholar and former White House official—did not know that prayer was important to me at all. Millions of people knew my life story, yet they had no idea that I prayed, no inkling that prayer made a difference in my life.

I began to wonder how many of the women I looked up to were also privately powered by prayer. So I set out to interview strong women—some well-known, others not—to find out what they knew about relying on prayer in the real world.

What I learned from these incredible women was more sacred, more practical, and more uplifting than anything I could have imagined. I began to wonder if I would be able to put such an ethereal feeling into words. But the words of the women themselves gave me a guide. The concrete details they were able to share about their prayer lives inspired me to try new ways to pray and to focus more on what matters most.

In the pages that follow, I also have shared the ups and downs of my own prayer evolution as the thread that binds the stories of other women together. As a whole, this book is a spiritual quilt of women's lives you can wrap around yourself. Their stories had such a profound impact on me, and on my life in prayer, that I truly feel I am not the same person I was when I began this project. Your life may never be the same again, either, after reading them.

I interviewed women from their twenties to their nineties living in the Northeast, the South, the Midwest and the West. African-American, Asian, Romanian, Rwandan and Caucasian women were included. I spoke to conservatives and liberals. They were athletes, beauty queens, politicians, TV producers, poets, doctors, and, of course, mothers.

Despite their differences, their prayer lives were similar. They prayed anywhere and everywhere: in cars, bathrooms, beds, gyms, planes, and more. They talked to God in normal words, sometimes even out loud.

I've learned that prayer is simply the desire to be closer to God. God is always there for us, reaching out to connect. We are the ones who turn away, get busy, and tune out God. Prayer is what brings us back into alignment—into oneness—with God.

Conversations about prayer are rare. People can go to church together every day and never talk about how they pray. Husbands and wives can pray separately for a lifetime and never share the experience. Even in a prayer group, most people talk about what they are praying about, not how they actually pray.

On the rare occasions we do talk about prayer, it is usually with experts (such as ministers or scholars) who tell us what we should do or what we should feel. They can't help it. It is their job to be teachers. What makes this book a unique and incredibly nurturing experience is hearing real people open up and talk candidly about their prayers.

When you read this book, I believe you will begin to hunger for discussions about prayer, too. As a matter of fact, why don't you, right now, think of a friend or loved one with whom you can start to have this kind of discussion? Contact that person, work out a comfortable time and place to get together, and start talking about prayer! If you like, you can use the exercise I created for my prayer group (see p. 274) or use the discussion guide at www.howstrongwomenpray.com.

I can't guess what you will discover about yourselves, but I can predict that you will get closer to God.

In the meantime, sit down and relax. Get a cup of tea or coffee. Get out your journal if you want to write down any of the feelings that might come up for you as you read. Let's go on this journey together to meet twenty-seven extraordinary women who share their innermost feelings about their lives and prayer. The blessings available to us—and through us—are truly without limit.

HOW
STRONG
WOMEN
PRAY

PART I

FACING LIFE'S STORMS
WITH CHILDLIKE FAITH

Heather Whitestone McCallum

Heather Whitestone, a tall, green-eyed brunette, was competing in her first major pageant. As she stood poised in front of the judges, she felt confident that she had a chance to win. A talented ballerina, Heather had never let her hearing impairment keep her from living life to the fullest. But as she tried to answer the judges' questions she began to panic. She tried to keep smiling, but when they spoke they were not looking at her: not a problem for a hearing person, but Heather read lips. She couldn't understand what they were asking her. She stumbled over the answers and lost.

Heather cried to her parents, "I lost because I am deaf."

But her parents would have none of it. "No," they said, "you lost because you were dishonest. If you had told the judges you were deaf, they could have talked facing you so you could read their lips."

It was an important lesson for Heather. She returned to the pageant the next year. Her talent segment was a ballet performance to "Via Dolorosa," a song that she had never heard due to her disability. After a bout with meningitis, Heather lost her hearing at eighteen months old. She had to literally count the beats and memorize the rhythm of the music.

And this time, because she was honest about her hearing impairment, the judges kept their faces toward her when they talked and wrote down their questions if she didn't understand. Heather won the crown and became Miss America 1995.

When I was on the road as Miss America, one of my oldest friends contacted me with an important request. She was dying of cancer and wasn't sure how much longer she had to live. She asked me to pray for her, and of course I agreed.

I wasn't exactly sure what to do. Should I pray for a long time? Maybe I should fast? I decided that God was in charge of her life, and if it was time for her to leave the earth, praying for a long time wasn't the answer. I sat down and said to God, "My friend has cancer. I don't know what Your plan is for her life. I trust Your decision and I ask You to give her a peaceful feeling about whether she will die soon or not."

And that was all. It was a quick prayer. I called her and told her that, as she went through her dark valley, I had prayed for her. It was such a chaotic time for me. As part of my duties as Miss America I was traveling all over. My days were very long and I had little time for any personal life. So I didn't see her until months later. That was eleven years ago and today she still lives. She still tells others that my prayer saved her life.

I felt embarrassed by that. My prayer was not that fancy and didn't even last a long time. When I told her, she said it didn't matter because she strongly believed that God was there to hear my prayer and let her know that He would bless her with a longer, healthy life. She said my words made her day in the hospital.

This was an interesting experience for me because it showed me how much God cares about even my quick prayers. He loves them as much as my long prayers. He appreciates anyone who takes the time, even a few moments, to pray. The power of prayer is so simple. God shows me that through prayer He can do anything.

I feel like I should have a traditional prayer routine, but I don't. I usually talk to God about three times a day. When I am facing an obstacle or am upset or frustrated, sometimes I talk to Him ten times a day! I don't pray with a memorized, formal prayer that is always the same. I pray differently every day because I talk and listen to God like I do with my close friends. Sometimes my prayers last fifteen minutes; other times they last thirty minutes.

I usually pray in my room or bathroom, where I can be alone. And once or twice a week I go by myself to the beach or backyard and just listen to God's voice while I watch His view of nature. But at nighttime I pray with my boys—John, age six and James, age five—after we read a children's Bible. We pray out loud for about five minutes. Their prayers are usually sweet and sometimes they make me laugh because they're so cute. They usually laugh with me afterward and we kiss each other when we say good night to God.

I always look at God like He's my father, when I pray. I talk to Him like a daughter who wants to share her joy, her sorrow, and her concerns, or even wants to seek His advice on something, even about her clothes and weight. I ask God to teach me how to be a better wife, a better mother, and a businesswoman.

Other times, I pray like this: "God, thank You for being good to me. I'm here and listening. Please speak to my heart. I just want to sit on Your lap and listen to good things about myself from You. What do You like about me?" I'm like a daughter who desperately wants to hear loving words from her father every day!

Of course, like most people, I prayed differently when I was younger. I was pitiful when I was a kid! I asked God a thousand times to heal my deafness, make me a ballerina (He answered that prayer!) and to make my hair curly in a natural way. I hated the perm my mother did on my hair. That perm chemical was my torture because it smelled terrible for days! I did not seek Him for anything else until I was eleven years old. Then I started to ask God many other questions about life and His plan for my future.

If I had to choose one Bible verse that sums up how I feel about prayer and my relationship with God, it would be Jeremiah 29:11. It is always in my mind because so many times I think life is unfair. I don't know why some people are born deaf or with other disabilities and others are not. But the Holy Spirit challenges me to think of this Bible verse very often:

> For I know the thoughts that I think toward you,
>> saith the LORD,
> thoughts of peace, and not of evil,
> to give you an expected end. [Jeremiah 29:11 KJV]

I sit down and I say, "I come to You and ask You to guide me and give me the courage and comfort to take one step at a time. Please keep me in Your arms like a baby and help me to change myself for better. I trust this Bible verse You gave me."

I Love Sunday School!

I walked along the dusty dirt road, dragging my right leg with each step since the heavy brace kept my leg from bending. The growth in my right leg was stunted from birth, so I wore white, high-top orthopedic shoes with this metal brace providing a stilt to even up my legs.

I watched the dust and rocks scuff and dirty the white shoes I had polished only the night before. I hated wearing those ugly shoes that made me look crippled and deformed. Having to polish them only made it worse.

Being four years old, I had to struggle to keep up with my seven-year-old sister, April, on our way to church on Sunday. My six-year-old brother, Wayne, continually ran ahead, threw pebbles into bushes to flush the birds or climbed on the ruins of old houses that had been condemned to make way for the new freeway. Years later, once the freeway was built, we would no longer be able to walk to church at all.

The three of us kids walked straight up our dirt road over

a small hill and down the other side to a small, one-room, cinder-block non-denominational Christian church.

I loved Sunday school. My teacher, Gladys Sumpter, was a chubby, older woman who reminded me of my grandmother on my father's side, who was white. On the black side of the family, my mother's mother died before I was born, so my entire concept of "grandmother" was a chubby, white woman with glasses and curly gray hair.

In Sunday school, we had beautiful pictures of Jesus and the disciples with stories of their adventures. There were crafts to do, punch to drink, and cookies to eat.

I don't remember the exact day that I asked Jesus to come and live inside my heart. I think I did it every time they suggested it, just to be sure that He was still there.

Once, I got assigned a verse to say in the Christmas pageant at church. My stepfather, Paul, helped me to memorize it. My real father, Lee, had left my mother while she was pregnant with me. Paul tested me on my Bible verse over and over until I could say it by heart without thinking. It seemed very odd to me that I still went blank on stage and couldn't recite my verse no matter how hard I tried. My face flushed hot with humiliation.

Going to Head Start preschool was a lot like Sunday school, but the stories weren't as good. My sister, April, had taught me to read already, and I was bored a lot. They had milk instead of punch.

Since my mother worked all day as a teacher, Paul picked me up from preschool. He was retired. He was very, very old. He combed his thinning gray and white hair back over his bald spot.

When we got home, I would go into my room to put away my sweater and stuff. Often, he would come into my room.

I shared my room with my sister, but she was still at school, as was my brother.

When Paul came into the room I knew to lay on the bed. He would take off my clothes and play with certain parts of my body with his fingers, and even his tongue. Sometimes he took off all his clothes and I was supposed to play with his parts, too. The very first time he came in my room, he put his mouth between my legs. It scared me so much, I howled and struggled. But he held me down until I got used to it. I learned to help as much as I could. I wanted to be a good girl.

I still wanted to be a good girl when my mother told me they were going to cut off my leg. She explained that I would get a brand new leg that would allow me to walk more normally.

"I'll be able to wear normal shoes?" I asked. "Any color? Both feet touching the ground?" She nodded. "Great," I said, "cut it off!"

Months passed on the third floor of the Shriner's Hospital for Crippled Children in Los Angeles. My world narrowed to three long, dim corridors with graying white walls, medicinal smells, wheelchairs, and the twenty other girls on the ward.

For a five-year-old, six months feels like forever. Halloween, Thanksgiving, my birthday, and Christmas all passed in the hospital with no home-cooked meals, no sister and brother, and no parents, unless the holiday fell on a Sunday. None did.

When my mother and stepfather tried to sneak upstairs to give me a cake for my birthday one Saturday, the hospital unceremoniously threw them out. As punishment, they were barred from visiting on Sunday. No one told the ward nurses or me what happened, so Sunday morning I dressed up like the other kids, let the nurses primp up my hair, and waited for my parents to come. Since my sixth birthday was the day before, I just knew they would bring me a present, and maybe a cake. We all waited eagerly with eyes wide, like puppies in a pound hoping to be claimed by the next passerby. As each parent came in to claim a waiting child, I watched and watched.

"Maybe the next one," I kept thinking, until finally, visiting time ended. I was exhausted from hours of waiting, straining on the edge of my bed, and hoping for my parents to come and celebrate my birthday. All the loneliness, isolation and pain of surgery I'd felt welled up in me and poured out in a torrent of tears. I lay on my hospital bed, a sodden heap of primped-up curls; a cold hollow spot inside. Through this and other experiences, I learned that having feelings and caring about people meant getting hurt. I wanted to stop feeling anything.

The physical pain of surgery and therapy was almost a welcome distraction from the routine loneliness and boredom. The amputation left me with a rounded stump of a leg, which was a bit longer than the thigh of my other leg. Sharp, stabbing pains, called phantom pains, shot through my nonexistent foot. By day I somehow was able to ignore it. Some nights, however, I would awaken to a nurse shaking me to stop me from screaming in my sleep.

To cope with the depressing realities of life, I not only controlled my emotions, I escaped into other worlds through books and stories. At age six, I powered through an entire set of Dick–and–Jane readers and polished off two or three spelling chapters a week while the hospital's schoolteacher sat back aghast.

I was drawn back to reality by trips to the physical therapy room. It was different from every other part of the hospital because it was filled with brightly colored pillows, stuffed animals, toys, and games. But I spent agonizing hours in that sunny room, trying to toughen up the end of my stump by pushing on a bathroom scale perched on a pile of books.

Finally, the time came for me to go home. My mother had to work, so Paul came to pick me up from the hospital on the day I was discharged. The nurses gave me a real dress to wear instead of the loose cotton outfits we'd worn every day. My hair was pulled into pony tails and hung in shiny black curls. I had one crutch and my new leg, which was made entirely of wood with metal hinges at the knee. It looked like Pinocchio's leg.

The excitement of going home and new clothes faded in the presence of my first real pair of shoes. All of my attention was focused on drinking in the beauty of seeing normal shoes on my own feet. During the two-hour drive from Los Angeles back home to San Diego, I didn't look out the window, but stared at the incredible shoes on my feet. I had picked them out myself: dark blue suede, with windows cut into the top part like stained glass. Red stitching edged the cutouts and circled the entire shoe, attaching it to a black waffle sole. They were, without a doubt, the most beautiful things I had ever seen.

When my mother got home from work, she watched me walk with my new wooden leg and admired my blue suede shoes. She took a picture of me in the backyard showing off my new leg. Then Mom gave me a brochure she had found with a silhouette of an amputee on a ski. It read, "If I can do this, I can do anything." I put the brochure in a box that held my special treasures: a lock of my dog's hair and a rock from the Grand Canyon.

Ann Marie Moloney

NYPD Detective Ann Marie Moloney was alone in a section of the city where she had never been before. Still a rookie and wearing her brand-spanking-new cop uniform with a nice, shiny radio, she walked down Jamaica Avenue in Queens, New York, a predominantly black, working class neighborhood. While she felt right at home where she grew up, just a few subway stops away, in a predominantly black and Hispanic area of Jackson Heights, here, with her never–used gun holster and her high-gloss shiny shoes, residents eyed her with suspicion.

Suddenly, she stopped in her tracks. She could hear a woman screaming at the top of her lungs. Everyone wondered . . . What will the rookie woman cop do?

Adrenaline rushed through her body. Ann Marie was on edge—tense, desperately trying to figure out where the screams were coming from. Activity surrounded her: kids played basketball, buses rumbled back and forth, cars darted in and out of traffic. As the knots in her stomach grew larger, she hoped the screams were not too close or too dangerous. Only a few weeks out of the academy, she still waited to be partnered up.

The screams were getting louder, closer. Suddenly, a car came screeching around the corner. A woman leaned out of the passenger side window—her whole upper body out of the car—she held a fourteen- or fifteenth-month-old baby by the leg and arm. The baby was clearly not breathing.

As soon as the mother spotted the uniform, the car skidded over and the woman thrust the baby into Ann Marie's arms. Her eyes were wide open, expectant. She looked at Ann Marie as if she was the only hope on the entire planet. She screamed hysterically in Spanish, *"Por Favor! Por Favor! Ayudame!"* Please, please! Help me! Make my child breathe again.

Being from a large Irish family, holding babies was second nature to Ann Marie. Her CPR skills were up to date.

She instantly laid the baby on the ground and started giving it mouth to mouth. As soon as she got the baby to breathe, Ann Marie began screaming in her radio for an ambulance. All formality was out the window—she spoke no code numbers into the radio. Six cars pulled up with lights flashing and sirens blaring. The mother was crying and kept saying, *"Gracias, Gracias,"* over and over.

I think that was probably one of the scariest moments in my life. I was only in my early twenties. I remember sitting in the back of the patrol car on the way to the hospital and my heart was pounding—*boom-boom-boom-boom*. I was feeling so high and thinking, "God, this is great! Look what we did!"

But then an older, more experienced cop burst my bubble, saying, "One thing you need to know, Kid: You never put your mouth on that kinda kid. You don't know what kinda disease you're gonna get."

I said, "I don't understand."

And he said, "You'll learn."

I was devastated. I didn't understand what he meant. I saw a child. I didn't see black. I didn't see white. I didn't see Latino. I was just shocked that he was implying that this child's life wasn't worth it. He thought the possibility of my getting sick wasn't worth trying to revive this child because the child was not a little white, Irish child.

I didn't think about any of that. I just went and I did what I had to do. How do you find the strength in a situation like that? It's God. Who else could it be?

There's no question that I had the courage to do it because I trusted and I knew that He was going to help me. If that poor child had passed away, obviously I would have been devastated, but at least I know personally that I did everything I could to make sure that baby was okay.

You need God backing you up, especially on this job. He's the strongest backup I'll ever have. If you don't believe in Him, if you don't have faith, how do you go out there?

I think about all those firefighters and cops that ran into the buildings on 9/11. As part of the ceremonial unit, I was responsible for organizing the funerals for and burying twenty-three police officers. Many of them were my close friends and co-workers.

God was behind those officers. They trusted that God was going to do the right thing, whether He was going to call them home or whether He was going to let them go back to their families here on earth. They had enough belief and strength in God that they went ahead and tried to do the best they could to help. You need God in your life as a cop. If you don't, how do you have the strength?

You have to understand that you are a tool and that God is going to use you. If you are willing, He will put you in the path of people that need your help. He understands. He loves. He cares. That's why I've been a police officer for over seventeen years. I truly believe that He works through me.

When you're a police officer, people turn to you and trust you. They almost look at you like you are God when they need help. And some days you can feel drained of the God in you. People just want you, and they want you and they want you.

When I go home and I'm drained and exhausted, and my child crawls into my lap and says, "Mommy, I love you so much." That's my reward. God gave me these beautiful children. My reward every night is to go home and to have a little hand clasp my big hand. I find such companionship in the silence. My children don't have to say a word.

My kids have always seen me pray. They've always seen some form of prayer in our house. The way to teach someone to pray is through your own actions. They watch me and they want to be like me. Consistency is important. No matter what, we will always go to church at the same time, every Sunday. No matter what, we will always pray every morning and every night.

My parents came from Ireland in the 1950s. My kids watch my parents pray too. I'm not saying we're the greatest family on the face of the earth, we obviously have disagreements, and some days we just want to strangle each other!

If we argue, if Liam pulls his sister's hair, or if Saoirse smacks him in the head—and that happens, because they're kids—prayer is always there. The children have always had religious toys to play with and you'll see pictures of Jesus around the house. There has always been a children's Bible in almost every room. I had a whole box full. I love children's Bibles because you get a good story and a giggle without all the thees and thous.

On 9/11, we went downtown after the towers fell to give assistance. I got there within the first hour or so, but there was nothing there. From three to four or five blocks away, all you saw were shoes. Literally, people ran right out of their shoes. Hundreds of shoes were all over the place. It was like somebody had plucked the people up and just put them somewhere. It was just outrageous. We were trying to bring water down there, but it was so chaotic that we had to come back to my post at the police academy a few blocks away.

We didn't know what was going on. We had radios, but our cell phones were dead. Most of us were on the street, we weren't manning the TV. All we heard was that the Pentagon was being attacked and something had happened in Pennsylvania. Rumors were flying around like crazy. I thought the world was coming to a crashing end. I had no idea what was going on in the rest of the country.

Once we were able to get our land lines up at the academy, that's where everybody came. It became like an emergency center. We're across the street from Cabrini Hospital, so we were waiting for any dead or wounded to be brought back. We had set up all these beds for a triage center downstairs in our gymnasium. We were just waiting for them to bring anybody from downtown—firefighters, cops, civilians. They didn't bring a single person in.

It was devastating to see those empty beds. I didn't expect

that because I figured "When these beds load up, boy, it's going to be sad to see all these people in here injured." But not one person came. That was worse than what I had imagined.

Most of the people who were coming back from downtown were completely covered in soot, so they were being decontaminated outside. They were just being hosed off and given clothing. All modesty went away. They just changed in the street to get out of their clothes.

Within twenty-four hours, churches began to respond. These beautiful women—from down South, from upstate, from out West, from the Midwest—came in vans. They brought food and clothing.

We spent probably the first three or four weeks alternating on and off, going down to the pile to dig. And every now and then a bell would sound, a little siren, or a horn that would mean someone found remains. Everyone would stop while they brought the person or the remains out, covered in an American flag. The whole thing was very strange and unusual.

Kids gave us stuffed animals and other gifts so we wouldn't be frightened at night—their favorite Elmo toy or a Power Ranger blanket. They were giving up their blankies! They would hand you the only thing that they knew that kept them comfortable at night. You would get this old, torn up blankie with a little scrawled note, "Be strong," or "God loves you." Or you'd get a crooked flag with two red stripes from a three year old that said, "God bless America."

In this horrible situation, the strength was coming from little kids, and do you know why? Because God used those children to give us adults hope and strength. Those kids have complete faith in us as police officers and firefighters and we have to draw our faith from them. It's such a beautiful circle that's been created by God for us. When you don't recognize these things in life, you miss out.

I still suffer from a variety of medical problems because of all the dust I inhaled in the first weeks after 9/11. I've had my gall bladder removed. And after extensive therapy at the New York Rescue Workers Detoxification Center, my various lung conditions and the ability to sleep were greatly improved. I don't have to take antihistamines every day anymore. But the Center, which has helped so many officers recover from the effects of 9/11, is still struggling for funding (see www.nydetox.org).

When I was on patrol I did see a lot of bad stuff. But, from bad, good sprouts all over. Like the time when a young girl was hit by a car as she was walking home from a birthday party in Staten Island. Her parents made the choice to donate her organs. Out of that accident, out of that tragedy—the funeral, the wake, the burial, going to the cemetery, all of this—she was able to help seven different people live a longer life. There is an eleven year old out there with her corneas, and another kid with her liver. So good came out of it. You have to look at it in a different way. If you see only the bad, you're going to shut down.

If I had to give any advice about praying it would be to never stop. Just keep learning. I would also say just listen. If you don't have prayer in your home right now, that's fine. If you weren't raised with prayer, seek it out. Spend half an hour, or twenty minutes, each day by yourself, whether you're sitting in your car, waiting for an appointment, or at home.

Even if you think you don't know how to pray, just being silent is praying. Gardening is praying to God. Singing is praying to God. Some people don't understand that. They think that they have to go through this whole religious education in order to be close to God. But God is close to us. We're the ones that push Him away.

I think that if I could go back twenty years, I would like to recoup a couple of years or days or moments where I struggled through a lot of things that were going on in my life. Instead of turning to God or going to church and praying, I acted like I needed to make that decision by myself. I didn't even think about asking, Hey, can I have a little help? Hey, can I have a little support? That's why my favorite Bible verse is: "I can do all things through Christ who strengthens me" (Philippians 4:13 KJV).

Leaning on the Lord

BONNIE'S STORY

When I was eleven years old, I joined my brother and sister, who were already scholarship students at the Bishop's School for Boys and Girls, a fabulous private school in La Jolla, California. The manicured lawns and elegant buildings looked more like an ivy-league campus than a high school. I wore black–and–white saddle shoes with a green-and-blue plaid uniform and a starched white shirt. Everything whispered "money" and "success." For me, it was stressful to be there. I didn't fit in with the rich, blonde, beach crowd.

Inside the chapel on campus, I found refuge. It was dark, cool, and somewhat musty. The chapel had no windows. Either side of the long narrow aisle was covered in dark wood: wood pews, wood paneling to the ceiling, and carved wooden seats at the back were built into the walls. Walking up the polished stone floor to the altar, I genuflected in front of a burst of color: cloth draping infused with gold thread, giant candlesticks, and all the ceremonial gear of the Episcopal faith—almost as elaborate as a Catholic Church.

Here I let go of everything from the outside world. Here, I forgot about how much I hated being humiliated in physical education because I couldn't run as fast as the other kids. In the chapel I could distance myself from the times when I had to get in the pool, take off my leg and and let kids see how my stump of a leg looked like a giant turkey drumstick. I wasn't one of the popular girls.

I worried about many things. I worried about studying hard to keep up with all these privileged kids who had been in private schools all their lives. I worried about whether Mom could afford to pay for the school supplies, textbooks, and uniforms we needed. It was always a struggle. She borrowed money to pay our tuition and we were always running out. Once we were thrown out of school and publicly humiliated a few days before exams for not paying bills. The stress made my stomach hurt. I begged my mother not to send me to Bishop's.

At home, my mother, Ruby, was fighting more and more with my stepfather, Paul. Loud arguments happened more frequently. Once Mom broke all the dishes. I know it wasn't very Christian of me, but I fantasized about killing Paul by soaking his vitamins in rat poison and then putting them back in the bottles. I figured, as an eleven year old I probably wouldn't even go to jail. Although he stopped molesting me when I was seven and I had blocked out all the memories of it, I still had some pent up rage toward him.

I joined the altar guild so that I could spend more time in the chapel. I helped Father Edelman prepare the Eucharist and put on his robes. There was a lot of bowing, kneeling, and reciting of prayers, all of which I found soothing and comforting. I liked lighting the candles in the ritualistic order.

I met Barbara Warmath in altar guild. She was tall and athletic, with her thick brown hair cut into the Dorothy Hamil wedge that was in style. We observed the Episcopalian rituals together. She reached out to befriend me even though I wasn't very good at being a friend. I didn't share my feelings, invite her to do things, or stay in touch when she later left Bishop's. I was too bottled up to let anyone get close. Still, her kindness calmed and reassured me.

I wanted more of the peace I felt in the chapel. I asked my mom for a silver cross on a chain that I started wearing under my uniform. I thought if I read the Bible cover to cover maybe I would find the answers. I gave up before finishing Genesis.

Dr. Suzanne Karefa-Johnson

Hospice physician Dr. Suzanne Karefa-Johnson went to bed one night. Around midnight, she woke up and thought the house felt very cold. She climbed out of bed and went upstairs to the boiler area and opened the door.

There she saw what looked like soot. Thinking it was strange, she recalled her parents were staying with her and wondered if she should wake her father to investigate. But then she had a feeling come over her: *No, no, it's okay.* Something told her to just get blankets, go back to bed and figure it out in the morning.

In the morning, Suzanne got up and woke her father. He looked at it and agreed that something was not right. "Oh, wow!" he said. "Something's happened here!" And he urged her to call the serviceman.

When the serviceman arrived he had a similar reaction. "Whoa, what's happened here?" he asked.

The serviceman investigated and explained that there had been an escape of gas. He told them, "If you had tried to do anything and light this thing last night, the whole house would be gone. I would have walked into nothing but powder and dust. In other words, you'd have gone up in smoke."

About six or seven months after my husband Kendrick died, I found myself asking a lot of questions about death. When death comes close, all of a sudden you start to look at all of these things that you just rattled off to comfort other people and you start to really think about them.

Where is my loved one? Is Kendrick in heaven? What is that like, Lord? So one night for some reason I just had to question. I said, "Lord, I really want to know if what I believe is true. Is the spirit part of Kendrick is still here? I really want to know about that. Is that the way it really is?"

When the serviceman told us that the house could have blown up, immediately, I thought back to my prayer. I had a sense of inner knowing that this was the answer to my prayer. I had been a very dependent wife in terms of that kind of thing. Kendrick fixed everything and I was clueless. I could see Kendrick going to the Lord and saying, "Okay, Lord, there's a problem here with the heater and Suzanne needs to know about it. So let's wake her up and let's have her figure out that it's there. But let's not have her do anything about it. Lord, I know you made her, but I know this woman. I've been by her side for so many years and I know she'll bring this house down if she tries to fix it. Just put her back to bed and in the morning my father-in-law will handle it."

I could see and hear that clearer than anything. I knew that was my answer to prayer. I felt Kendrick's spirit protecting me, close to me. I know that I can't prove it to anyone else, but I knew it inside. The message got through loud and clear.

As a hospice physician, I see every day that there's a lot of work to be done around dying. Those who have a conscious death, and are aware of that trajectory of that last time on earth, really have a blessing that a lot of people don't have.

If you're suddenly hit by a car you have no time to reflect. Or, if you're dying of HIV/AIDS somewhere in Africa, you may have time, but there are no resources to help you walk that path. You still have to feed your kids.

We live in a very blessed situation here in this country where we can come into hospice, bring in the social worker, bring in the spiritual person, and have a physician and the nurse, etc. That's not the way most of the world meets their death.

What happens most often in this situation is that there's not a lot of room for pretense and superficiality. The first thing you lose is all of the "could be's." When death is imminent, you're dealing with what is and what has been.

There's a real sharpening of reality. And along with that, hopefully, there comes a kind of defining of what is really important. People who are dying initially approach prayer with the patterns they have been taught. For example, they may be very fearful if they grew up with a very judgmental God. Or they have a sense of comfort and companionship along the journey if they were raised to feel a sense of the presence of God.

Then there are those who come from a sense that "This is all there is, and no one's been in it with me before, and no one's going to be in it now, and I'm doing this on my own." And those people will tell you they're not spiritual, they're not religious . . . they have a very mechanical way of approaching life. They've lived their life and this is it.

Typically, as people get closer to death, a lot of defenses start disappearing. I equate the dying process with the process of packing to go on a journey. Where you are going is not for me, as your physician, to tell you, but you are going on a journey. You know that you are leaving this earth.

Your defenses go down because you are husbanding your energy. People intuitively know dying is work, just like laboring to bring babies into this world is. You start to conserve your energy.

The dying start to disengage from external life. Partly it's because they're now bed-bound and they can't go shopping anymore or go out and see the latest movie.

On another level, they start to disengage from relationships. Families find this really, really hard to deal with. You come in and they just want to talk about their medication or they just want to talk. They don't say, "How are you? How was your day? What's going on?"

I don't know that I'm right, but I see that they need their energy to go through this very hard work of letting go of life. And that means that they no longer have the energetic resources to bring to the table the way that you and I do to get through our very active, energy-expending daily life in the external world.

As that happens, people seem to become more sensitive to other things. I think it's somewhat akin to people who have impairment of one of more of the senses. The other senses become more acute. What I sense is that people, as they start to disengage from some of that externalization of life, become much more perceptive of what seems to be going on at a level that is not one at which you and I live, at least consciously.

As people get closer to death, that becomes more and more pronounced. My experience is that a lot of the requests for prayer happen solely early on in that "dying process" from the person who's making the journey. The person making the journey gets less and less interested in you praying for them or even with them *per se*. Again, I can't say this categorically, but that's my experience. Prayer seems much more internally focused. I believe they are doing their own prayer process. Many times they aren't necessarily very verbal anymore by that time, so it's hard to know exactly what's going on.

People start to do what we call "angel watching" when they lie down on their beds and you can see them looking at the ceiling. Their eyes are sort of tracking things and they're kind of looking around the room. And then, people start to talk about past loved ones who have already passed over: "Uncle So-and-So is here." Or, an eighty-five year old talking about, "Oh, Mom is here."

In medicine, "terminal delirium" is what it is called. But I choose to think that they really are starting to cross over. I think the veil between individual spirit and God is not there as thickly as it is in this time and space continuum where we live. There is already that sense of communication and that sense of oneness, such that there is no need for external prayer the way that we do prayer.

As they get closer to departure, the family may be praying, "Let them not be in pain. Let them be in peace. May they go straight to heaven." But I don't find that the dying do a lot of that kind of praying, or even ask for a lot of that kind of praying.

I sense the dying pray much more from a sense of one-ness with God. They are praying by the very definition of death, which, in medicine, the term is "expiring," letting out the breath, the breath of life, which, to me, is God's spirit. That is the most final and beautiful prayer because it is that person's final utterance as they leave this physical body and transition to that next phase. And to me, what more power-ful prayer is there than that?

I learn a lot from the dying. Having sat with so many people who die, I would defy anyone to tell me that they know at which point that door closes, in terms of a chance for "salvation."

To me, if you look biblically, breath is God's Spirit. God breathed on the once dry bones in Ezekiel. God "breathed" into Adam and made man. So breath is that part of God that makes us alive.

I learned that lesson so powerfully when I turned the corner fourteen years ago and walked into our living room at home. I looked across the room and I saw my husband, Kendrick, dead on the sofa. He could have been sleeping, but the difference was that his spirit had gone. It was no longer Kendrick. It looked like Kendrick, he had his same clothes on, his hair was the same, but that was not Kendrick anymore. What had changed? I believe his spirit, his vital force, had left.

Spirit is life-giving breath. What I'm saying is, as you expire, that is your last utterance of giving back to God that which God breathed into you to make you a living being. It's the ultimate prayer.

Working with people who are dying has not made me a somber person. In fact, the older I get, the more joy and freedom I feel in my relationship with God. I used to pray in a very traditional, serious way with a strict routine. I read the Bible all the way through several times. But now I pray in a less orthodox way: I dance. I never feel closer to God than when I'm dancing. I dance all over the house like other people sing in the shower. I choreograph movements for the Lord's Prayer.

When I am dancing I am so aware of an opening to God, God's spirit flowing through me and an infilling of joy. If there are blocks in my connection with God, dancing can be a very cleansing, liturgical process, too. When that happens I have really wept with dancing.

Prayer, to me, is the process that puts one in communion with God. For me, that is the bottom line of prayer. The times when I've been most aware of that communion, that oneness with God, are while dancing. I feel pure joy, which to me is this awesome experience that kind of wells up through my being. I take the position that much of our disease stems from a lack of conscious connection with God and a lack of experiencing joy and well-being.

From the dying I learn to focus less on the external world and more on complete communion with God. Facing death in a spiritual way is all about learning to focus on what really matters. The dying teach me to treasure each moment I have to live, to love, to heal, and to grow.

Departures

The car rolled silently through the fog in Oregon. I looked out the window, fascinated by the leafless trees. Growing up in San Diego, we never experienced the temporary death of trees during winter. They looked like lace against the sky. The bleak, gray day was perfect for my father's funeral. I was twelve. I hadn't known him at all.

He left before I was born and my mother never let him visit us. My mother said he was dangerous and unstable. He had epilepsy and refused to take his medicine. The seizures became worse and worse, affecting his brain. He had physically attacked several people, including his own mother, my Grandma Leah, who he loved dearly.

Just before the funeral, Mom told us that he had come and watched us from far away a few times. He'd watched us on a playground at school or playing in our front yard. But he hadn't lived in San Diego, so I don't think he saw us much.

Grandma Leah was at the funeral. She was the only person

I knew in my father's family. The rest of the St. John family, Uncle Lynn, Aunt Laura, and my grandfather Lloyd, didn't want anything to do with my mother or the three of us kids. They didn't bring any of our cousins to the funeral because they didn't want to let them find out there were black people in the family. Aunt Laura and Uncle Lynn were polite to our faces, but my grandfather would not so much as look at me, Wayne, or April.

Before marrying Lloyd St. John, Grandma was Leah Barnhardt. There were several Barnhardt's living in Oregon, including her brother Dave and his wife, Carmen, and Aunt Olive. The color difference didn't matter to them and they embraced us as family, just like Grandma did. We met their kids, our cousins, and they took us to see snow and throw snowballs. We had a big family dinner at Dave and Carmen's house. It was easy to forget the cruelty of the St. Johns in the midst of the loving Barnhardts.

On the day of the actual funeral, we all went to the local church. I didn't hear a word of the service. Everyone was crying. As his daughter, I felt I should be crying, too. Yet I didn't feel anything. Nothing. I wracked my brain trying to feel sad somehow.

I remembered gifts, which came sporadically for Christmas or birthdays. I never liked his gifts—they were books that were too hard to read or a toy for a toddler when I was in fifth grade. He always messed it up. I felt even worse knowing I didn't like his gifts and I wasn't crying at his funeral.

Finally, I thought about him standing outside a playground, perhaps watching us play through a chain–link fence. I realized that even though he'd sent bad presents and was never around, he did love us. I focused on his love for us until I finally managed to squeeze out a few tears. Then I felt better.

Afterward, we went to the graveyard to put the box in the ground. It was on a hill overlooking a green valley below with forests broken by farms and country houses. Rain fell, turning the leafless trees dark black against the gray fog. Compared to living in the city, in San Diego, this place seemed to me so quiet, peaceful, and green. It felt like heaven. As we walked amid the gravestones, Aunt Olive pointed out other members of the Barnhardt family.

"Look, there's Olive Barnhardt!" Wayne said suddenly, looking at Aunt Olive as though she were a ghost.

Indeed, there was a tombstone carved with her name. It was part of a large double slab of marble that stretched across her husband's grave next door. She explained her spot was empty and waiting for her. We saw the blank spot where the date of her death would be carved.

At first, I thought it was spooky to see your own grave. Then I looked around at the view for miles in every direction, the fresh air, and deep peace. Maybe it was nice to know where you were going to end up.

A year after the funeral, my brother, my sister, and I came home from Bishop's School in our uniforms to a house that seemed more than silent. Our stepfather's car wasn't in the driveway. We looked at one another. Then April reacted first, leading the way to our parents' bedroom. She opened the closet.

"Look, his clothes are gone," she said. My heart skipped a beat. Could it be true? I opened a drawer: empty. We went into his study. The desk was clear, drawers empty.

"Hallelujah!" I cried out. We whooped and hollered for

joy. It was like a dark cloud hanging over the house was removed.

With Paul gone, my mother became the lively, funny person we had seen so little of in recent years. She threw parties for the students from the school where she worked as a vice principal. We had friends over. Instead of arguing, the sounds of music, laughter, and poetry filled the house. Instead of the bland, health-oriented food he made us eat with day–old bread and powdered milk, we had salsa and chips, real milk, and ribs on the barbeque. The long dark winter in our house became a perpetual California summer.

That was the year I turned away from God. Perhaps I thought I didn't need to escape into the cave-like chapel at school since Paul was gone. Or maybe it was later, when my mother had to pay college tuition for April, so she moved Wayne and me to a public school (but still on the rich side of town). No more chapel, no more altar guild. Or maybe I turned away from God when I hit puberty.

I felt freer than ever before: no Paul, no private school, no money worries about tuition and books. Over summer, I lied about my age to get a job in fast food so that I could buy contact lenses and new clothes. I was determined to start public school not as the nerdy crippled kid with glasses, but as a more outgoing person taking on new challenges. I didn't think I needed God anymore to make me feel better about life. I could start living my life on my terms—not avoiding it by burying myself in chapel or reading a Bible.

Colette Branch

As soon as she heard that a Category 5 storm, Hurricane Katrina, was in the Gulf and approaching New Orleans, Colette Branch, owner of an independent living services business for disabled people, says, "God told me: Get out of here. Don't wait. Don't sit around and wonder how. Whatever you have to do, leave." She and everyone who depended on her—nearly 100 severely disabled people and about 200 employees and their families—packed up and left town.

Colette's clients, who ranged in age from eleven to sixty-three, had disabilities including cerebral palsy, autism, Parkinson's, blindness, and some with combinations of each. Many couldn't even sit upright in a car. Getting everyone out of town was no simple matter.

Ten months before Katrina hit, as another potential hurricane threatened the area, the mayor of New Orleans issued a voluntary evacuation order. The poorly organized evacuation resulted in solid, wall-to-wall, unmoving traffic. People were stuck on the roads for hours. There were people hospitalized for dehydration and a busload full of elderly people caught on fire.

Colette took the false alarm as God's warning to prepare, whereas others were angry and felt even less willing to consider evacuating when Katrina entered the Gulf.

On Friday, two days before Hurricane Katrina made landfall, Colette told her staff, "We have to go." Because she prayed continuously and listened to God, she was able to construct an ark before the flood. She saved hundreds of lives.

Everyone told me not to worry about Katrina. They said, "On TV they say it's going in the other direction." But I knew it was coming to New Orleans. God told me, "Get out now. Don't wait."

When the last hurricane had threatened New Orleans, I prayed, "God, if you get me out of this one, I will never, ever stay and wait. As soon as I hear the warning I will prepare to go. I will never take a chance."

So when I started hearing warnings about Katrina, I told my staff to get the hurricane plan and that no matter what they said on TV we were leaving.

I told everyone that I would buy Six Flags passes for the clients and for the workers. I said to look on the bright side, if we left and it was unnecessary, we would consider it a vacation. That way, no matter what happened we were safe.

I decided to evacuate everyone in vans because trains and other forms of public transportation were not running. At the Enterprise rental office, I asked for fifteen vans, but they said I was not allowed to take them out of town. I lied and said I wouldn't; that I was renting the vans for fun. With a hurricane on the way, I knew they probably didn't believe me, but they gave me the keys anyway.

My attitude is that you deal with what is. And we did. I organized about fifty clients and thirty workers, including their children and spouses, into the fifteen vans, plus private cars and trucks. Together we drove six hours into Texas—cats, dogs, clients, and parents in tow. Everybody went with us, including two terriers, a Rottweiler, and a poodle.

Our caravan rode straight through without encountering one bit of traffic. Despite all the organization of bringing together such a large group of people, we left New Orleans by midday on Saturday. Most others didn't leave until Saturday night or Sunday morning.

I don't think most people understand what it was like for many of the residents of the Gulf Coast. You can't drive your car out of town if you have no gas. If you have no money for a hotel, where do you go? If you don't have any money, I can't make you have money. I can't say to you that you should have saved the money because you really don't have anything to save in the first place.

I did get reimbursements for the workers, but there is no reimbursement policy for evacuation costs. In our first week in Texas, hotel and food for the group traveling with me was $11,000. After that, we rented three seven-bedroom houses, where we stayed for two months. A local church came to our aid and furnished the houses complete with appliances, and even medical beds where we needed them.

I never worried about the money I was paying out for vans, food, and shelter for our group. One of my workers said to me, "Thank God we are with you." But I knew it was God we should thank that I had the money. Thank God that, over the years of doing this type of work, I was able to make money so that we had it then. Maybe this is why God gave me a profitable business.

People wonder how I ended up in the position to save so many people, especially disabled people. It really started a long time ago, when I was in school.

I was studying to be a special education teacher and I started working at the Methodist Home for Children, a refuge for abused and abandoned children. I tell everybody that it was the best job I ever had. I felt that for some strange reason God put me there. In school, my mind was always in a million different places and never in the place that it was supposed to be. If I was sitting in the classroom, I was the person looking out of the window the whole day. That was before Attention Deficit Disorder (ADD) was talked about. At work I felt more comfortable than in a school. I was better at handling the special needs children than I was at studying about it.

I eventually left college to work at Methodist Home full time, and that's where I met thirteen-year-old Trina. She was autistic, jumping on the bed and tearing up the room. Nobody wanted to be assigned to Trina. Since I was, at age nineteen, the youngest person on staff, they sent me in to work with her. We quickly bonded and I became her "momma." No one else could handle her at all.

I always did what I needed to do to help whatever child I was working with. I dealt with the issues and got them under control so they could be at peace with themselves. My job with Trina was to help her locate peace.

Everybody else in that home could talk, they could read, they could write, and they could do everything they needed to do. Trina couldn't talk, read, or write. And she was overweight—a size twenty-two.

They used her disability as an excuse for everything: She's lying on the floor because she's autistic. She eats too much because she's autistic. I told them, "She's doing that because y'all are letting her do it. You know why she won't get off the floor? You never asked her to get off the floor."

Trina is autistic but she has very, very good understanding. Because she had a disability nobody else wanted to sit down and talk to her like a person. Nobody wanted to take the time to learn whether she could understand something. It was much easier to make excuses for her.

The Methodist Home was licensed only to house kids up to the age of fourteen. As soon as Trina turned fifteen, she had to leave. The trouble was, she had nowhere to go.

I was so attached to her that, when it was time for her to leave, I left, too. I resigned my job, went through training, and became a therapeutic foster care parent so that I could take her home with me.

My mother pointed out that I didn't have a house. "You live with me," she said. So I went out and rented a condo. Then I had to confront the people who ran the foster program. They said, "You're too young to do it. You're not married. You don't have any kids of your own. You can't take her."

But I was determined. I told them, "I can and I will." I was going to make a better life for Trina.

Growing up, my Dad always gave me the same advice whenever I had a problem. He would say, "Child, I tell you, the Lord will work it out. Just pray on it." And I prayed and prayed that I could find a way to get approval to take Trina home.

My conversations with God are just like talking to a human being, the same as talking to anyone. It's just a simple routine of asking God to help me or to show me what to do. It can be as simple as: Lord, help me. I don't drop to my knees at a certain time of day, but I'm always asking the Lord to guide me in the direction that He chooses. If something important is not going to work out, I just get a sense or . . . a feeling from Him about what I should do.

I was successfully guided through the process of finding an apartment and convincing the authorities to let me take care of Trina. I was twenty-one and Trina was fifteen when we moved in together. I tutored several other foster children after school to make extra money over my stipend to care for Trina.

Once Trina turned eighteen, I started to worry that if something happened to me there would be no one to care for her. I researched and researched until I found a program that allowed her to have her own place with independent, assisted living in the community.

This means she will never in her life ever have to be institutionalized again.

This was the beginning of starting my business providing independent living assistance to people of all ages and disabilities. I love them, respect them and care for them as if they were members of my own family. I am now married with my own children, and my family and my parents still care for and love Trina, even though she lives in her own apartment.

I learned at an early age, there is no price tag on a human life. Having Trina around has allowed my kids to grow up and understand that everybody isn't the same, but you can treat everybody nicely. People are different and they have exceptional things about them, but it doesn't mean that they are any less than anybody else.

Living in the World

As tenth grade began, I turned away from God and embraced my life and myself. I left behind the geeky glasses, school uniform, and frizzy ponytails. With money from my summer job, I permed my hair straight, got contact lenses, and bought a selection of clothes for school that emphasized my figure and covered up my prosthesis. I learned to use a curling iron and makeup. I arrived at public school as a new me.

Instead of avoiding water sports, I signed up for a two hour PE class involving sailing, water skiing, windsurfing, and other water sports. I soaked up adventure and threw caution to the wind.

The best surprise of all at Mission Bay High School was Barbara Warmath. Her mother had pulled her out of Bishop's School the year before and we had lost touch. But here she was!

Barb never turned away from God like I did. Her whole life she has stayed close. After graduating from college she joined the Peace Corps. Years later, I visited her and her family while they volunteered at a Christian camp to help refugees.

For my birthday, Barb showed up at school with a certificate for me that she drew on a piece of notebook paper. "One week of skiing over Christmas vacation," it read. Her smile and enthusiasm wouldn't take no for an answer.

Without a friend like Barbara, I would have gone a different way. In my struggle to find confidence and an identity, I probably would have tried to party, drink, and maybe even get into drugs. I wanted to be popular.

But she offered a different kind of excitement: skiing. Barb changed my life, despite how different we were. She is white; I'm black. She was from La Jolla, the rich side of town; I was bused in twenty-five miles from near the Mexican border. She was on the tennis team; I was exempt from PE after having another surgery on my leg in high school. And yet, Barb turned to her one-legged, African American friend from the wrong side of the tracks and said, "Let's go skiing!" Her belief in me made me feel I could do it.

One of the other reasons I said yes to Barb's invitation was because of the brochure my mother had given me when I came home from the hospital after having my leg amputated. It had a picture on it of an amputee on a ski. Because of that picture, I knew that I could ski.

Ruby was a woman who believed in possibilities more than limitations. Her mother never went past the fourth grade and had two kids before age sixteen. Growing up, my mother didn't always have enough food to eat and had to put cardboard inside her shoes to cover the holes. Ruby's mother became an alcoholic and her boyfriends abused little Ruby physically and sexually.

But Ruby prayed and found strength from within. She was the first in her family to go to college. She'd earned her Ph.D. by the time I was twelve, and eventually worked her way up to being a principal of a school. You couldn't grow up with Ruby and make excuses about what you couldn't do.

I told her about Barb's invitation to go skiing.

"How will I find the special equipment for an amputee?" I asked. I knew I needed outriggers—poles with ski tips on the ends—because I saw them in the picture on the brochure.

"Here, look under sporting goods stores." My mother handed me a phonebook. She wasn't the kind of person to do it all for me. She was busy working and expected me to solve my own problems.

I called the first store on the list.

"I'm an amputee and I am going skiing. I need those poles with the ski tips," I said.

"Never heard of them," was the answer.

I called another store.

"Never seem 'em."

I called every store listed. Nothing.

I scratched my head. Maybe if I called a ski area?

"Yeah, I've seen amputees skiing here," I was told, "but I don't know where they get those things."

But Ruby's daughter couldn't give up. I asked everyone I knew for the next thirty days: my mother's friends, my friends' mothers. Finally, someone told me about a sports club for amputees, Amputees in Motion. The president of the club, Jerry Dahlquist, loaned me his own outriggers so that I could go.

I had decided to throw caution to the wind and try new things, like the water sports at school. Skiing, however, was a bigger challenge. It was one thing to go with a group of teachers and kids from school to the local aquatic center; going away to ski with Barbara was a much more daunting undertaking.

There were so many things to be afraid of. I had to go far away from home for a whole week to an expensive ski resort where I might not fit in. I was afraid I might not have enough money for expenses and be embarrassed. To ski, I would have to take off my leg, leave it at the bottom of the hill and use my outriggers like crutches with one ski. I would look weird. Worst of all, I might fail.

I was determined, however, to emerge from my shell and live life. I had become more outgoing at school. I had wind surfed and water skied. I wasn't going to back down from the opportunity to ski on snow.

When I got on the bunny hill, ready to do the beautiful and graceful turns I had seen on TV, I found that I could barely stand up on a ski, on a hill, on one leg. Immediately, I fell down.

I got up. In a few moments, I fell again. I bruised my leg from falling on my poles. My hands, in knit mittens, were already soaking wet and freezing. I was exhausted, cold and beat up. It was worse than anything I had imagined.

After some breaks and practice, I was able to actually move forward and stay standing. Then I picked up speed! In fact, I couldn't stop. On one leg, you can't snowplow to slow down. To stop myself I had to fall or crash into people on the hill.

The experience was nothing like the beautiful image I'd had of skiing gracefully down the hill. But I kept picking myself up. Finally, after three days of bruises and crashing, I learned to turn to the right and turn to the left with enough skill to stop myself. Suddenly I could ski! Unlike beginners on two legs, I never crossed my tips and crashed. I was perfect parallel skiing. I advanced to intermediate slopes.

Skiing was everything I had dreamed of and more. I felt the wind in my hair. I felt graceful and fast. I loved the fresh crisp air and the brightly colored ski clothes. I was hooked.

PART II

CLIMBING THE WORLD'S HIGHEST MOUNTAINS

Vonetta Flowers

Vonetta Flowers, a 2002 Olympic Gold medalist in bobsled, had dreamed of going to the Olympics from the time she was nine years old. But since she grew up in Birmingham, Alabama, she dreamed of being a track and field star—not a winter sports competitor.

So how did a black woman from Birmingham, Alabama, end up winning an Olympic gold medal in bobsled (and being the first African American winning winter gold)? When injuries snuffed out her track career she didn't become bitter. Instead, Vonetta took a risk and went in a new direction.

Vonetta believes her getting into the sport of bobsled was really a miracle. She was recruited from track by a leading bobsled driver and had been training only a year when she qualified for the Salt Lake City games.

While it took a great deal of courage to enter a world where none of the other athletes looked like her, bobsled takes courage for anyone. She recalls that the first time she tried it she was terrified.

"It felt like I had been placed in a trash can and thrown down a hill. It was so bumpy. My head was down between my knees and it was dark. My eyes were closed, I couldn't see anything, and I was scared out of my mind." After it was over she thought to herself, "What have I gotten myself into?"

Vonetta trained hard and became an excellent pusher. And with hard work, determination, and faith, the little girl from Birmingham was on her way to the Olympics.

Everything was going along perfectly. Then, two months before the Games, her driver had an abrupt change of heart and decided to pick a different partner to go to Salt Lake City. Vonetta was out.

It would have been easy to give up. But her husband, Johnny, kept reminding her, "God put you in this sport for a reason. Keep training." She was off the team and had no idea what would happen, but she continued to train anyway.

Vonetta acknowledges that to someone standing on the outside looking in, her decision to train when she was off the team seemed crazy. Focusing on reality, Vonetta should do one thing; but, instead, she listened to God in prayer. She trusted and decided to do something entirely different.

After two weeks of training as if she were still on the team, she received one phone call and then another, asking her to join different bobsled teams. She was back on track.

When Vonetta stepped up on the podium to accept the gold medal for the United States in bobsled at the 2002 Salt Lake City Olympics, few people were aware of the incredible odds she had to overcome to get there. If she had stopped training for those two weeks, she still might have gotten the offers to compete in the Olympics, but it is unlikely that she would have won the gold. She wouldn't have been ready. Her faith made the difference, and Vonetta had been working to strengthen her faith for a long time.

My faith was not always so strong. I went to church on Easter and all the typical holidays as a child, but that was it.

When I was competing in track I didn't believe in God. I felt like my talents were going to get me to the next level, not God. It was just me, me, me. But all of that changed when I met Johnny Flowers, my future husband.

Johnny is a preacher's kid. He went to church every day of the week. When he got to college, he was tired of church and took a break. But he soon realized that there was something missing in his life and he started going back. He invited me to come. Our relationship was good before, but it just got better once we started going to church together.

Through prayer, I learned that all of my gifts and all of my talents were from God, and that He was using me to do something with those talents. Now I know it's not even about me. It's all God.

Knowing that I can rely on God to get me through every situation is less stressful than when I was competing in track years ago and completely relying on myself. I started competing on faith, not fear.

During the Olympics, I specifically drew on a sermon from my pastor, Michael Moore, called "Winning the War Against Fear," and the verse from II Timothy 1:7, "For God did not give us a spirit of timidity, but a spirit of power, of love and of self-discipline" (NIV).

After I won the gold medal, I gave the credit and the glory to God. My husband said, "Not even Vonetta is strong enough to push that 450-pound sled and make it go that fast. Standing at the finish line, I knew that it was the prayers of a lot of people that allowed the team to do what they did."

Today, my husband and I get up before the kids and pray before the day gets started. I go downstairs into the basement and sit on a comfortable couch with my eyes open. I chose the basement because it is quiet, kind of closed in, and without any windows like other rooms in the house. Johnny goes to his office to pray.

It's not a specific pattern. It's just whatever comes to heart. I thank Him for seeing another day. I pray for my family. I ask God to get me through the day and to make me open to all the different things that happen. It's so important to pray every day.

In the evenings, we try to read the Bible together once the kids are settled, depending on where we are. A lot of times, if we can't do it together, Johnny will take the kids and do something with them while I read, and vice versa. We attend Bible study at our church when we're in town, or we just take our Bible with us on the road.

The way I look at it now, God has a purpose in everyone's life. At first, I thought my gold medal was to open the door, to help people to be more open-minded. A black person from Birmingham doing winter sports and winning a gold medal can change how people think—how white people think about black people and how black people think about themselves. Now more African Americans can consider taking their track skills into a new arena.

Looking back, I think there was an even bigger purpose to my involvement with bobsled. If I hadn't been in the sport of bobsled, I wouldn't have had the opportunity to be in Europe and meet the only doctor in the world who could perform the surgery to save my son Jorden's hearing. Now, we get so many e-mails and calls from people whose kids are suffering from the same problems that Jorden had and we can help them by sharing Jorden's story.

I had no way of knowing that winning the gold medal

would make all the difference in the world for my son because he wasn't even born in 2002 when I competed in Salt Lake City.

Right after the 2002 games, Johnny and I decided to start a family. It was not long before our twin sons, Jorden and Jaden, came along. After much prayer and planning, I decided to set my sights on the 2006 Olympics in Torino, Italy. Johnny signed on as my coach and we brought the twins with us on the World Cup racing circuit.

Although the kids were happy and healthy, their premature birth had caused hearing problems for Jorden. At about a year and a half, they confirmed that Jorden was getting no sound at all.

Cochlear implants and hearing aids don't work when you are missing the entire nerve responsible for hearing. There was one doctor in California performing the experimental surgery to replace the nerve with electrodes on the brain, but it was not yet FDA approved, even for adults. It turned out that the only doctor in the world performing auditory brain implant surgery on children was Dr. Vittorio Coletti in Italy.

We were e-mailing him, back and forth. He advised us that the best time to have this surgery for a kid was as soon as possible. We were not able to pick up and fly to Italy for a checkup. But we finally got a chance to meet him when we had a bobsled race in Cortina, which is a couple of hours away from Torino, the site of the 2006 Winter Olympics. We drove over, met him, and he evaluated Jorden.

If I wasn't racing, and bringing the whole family along, I don't know what we would've done. That evaluation was in February 2005. Dr. Coletti gave the thumbs up for Jorden— in his opinion, the surgery could allow Jorden to hear.

Furthermore, the doctor offered his services for free! We planned the surgery for December 2005, during a period when the family would be in Italy training for the upcoming 2006 winter games. Once again, it felt like God's hand was at work in our lives.

But then, two weeks before the surgery, Dr. Coletti informed us that since we weren't living there as residents and paying taxes, we would have to pay the entire bill for Jorden's hospital room and all the medicines, which could be up to seventy thousand dollars.

At that point, we were already in Europe. We didn't have that kind of money with us.

There I was, a few months from competing in the Olympics for the second time, my toddler is about to go in for brain surgery, and we needed to come up with a huge amount of money.

But we couldn't stress about it. That's where prayer comes in. We prayed and had faith it would somehow work out. We decided we would sell our house in Birmingham if we had to. I just kept training and moving forward on faith, not fear.

The surgery was scheduled for December 20, just before Christmas. *Good Morning America* decided to televise a Sunday morning story on me as I headed for the Olympics and Jorden headed into surgery. Because of the publicity, an Olympic sponsor—Allianz—stepped in and offered to pay the hospital bill for Jorden, which totaled nearly fifty thousand dollars by the time he was discharged!

My gold medal has meant so much more to me than winning a race. Without it, I don't know that I would have ever been able to get to Italy to meet Dr. Coletti. Would he have offered his services? Would I have had the publicity and a sponsor to pay for the surgery? My gold medal—which I won with prayer and faith—turned into a miracle for my son.

I came in sixth place at the Torino games. Yet I still feel like I won. I believe that praying as a family has strengthened us to meet the challenges that have come our way. When we are willing to be in a relationship and listen to Him, God can do great things!

Racing Against Life

I ran my fingers over the newspaper articles about myself in disbelief (and pleasure).

The National City Star News (6/11/81):

"Despite missing her right leg St. John's athletic ability probably exceeds that of most of her classmates, and she has two gold, a silver and three bronze medals to prove it. The medals are from the recent National Handicapped Ski Championships at Winter Park, Colorado."

Grover C. Crayton for the *Cleveland Call and Post* (8/81):

"I knew nothing about racing. No one was available to teach an amputee to race, so I began looking for books on the subject," says Bonnie. She gives a lot of credit for her success at the nationals (two gold

and one silver medal in cross-country and three
bronze in alpine events) to one of those books,
Warren Witherell's *How the Racers Ski*.
"Those around her give a lot of the credit to Bonnie.
She worked hard, skiing weekends, attending
school during the week and working in a drugstore weeknights to 'help support my habit.' If
enthusiasm, hard work and skill can do it, Bonnie
will be in Austria in 1984. She's already a winner."

Yes, I had worked hard to become a ski racer and win
six medals at my first national competition. I began skiing
with the amputee club where I borrowed the outriggers for
my first trip. By working in a drugstore after school from
4:00 p.m. to 9:00 p.m., Monday through Friday, I could
afford to ski on the weekend. I had no coaches, but entered
the NASTAR races, open to the public, in order to practice.

Cathy Gentile, a young amputee from Los Angeles, encouraged me to go with her to the national championships and
start racing against other amputees. Even if I didn't qualify
to race, she explained, I could enter a race clinic and learn
more about it.

I never expected to win medals at all. I managed to qualify for the top class of competition by only a split second. My
friend Cathy, a much better skier than I, was injured on the
first day and unable to compete. Since I managed to place
third in all three Alpine events, I felt as though I had won
her medals. I was stunned, but happy.

One of the best parts of being at a national race for the
disabled was seeing hundreds of disabled people together
for the first time in my life. They were not disabled people

feeling sorry for themselves, not a support group. When they dumped their artificial arms and legs, wheelchairs, and crutches at the bottom of the hill and went skiing, I felt as if I were in Lourdes, where people could touch the water and walk away healed.

And at night we danced! Cathy and I would curl our hair, put on makeup, and go to the main hotel hosting the event for a night of celebrating after each race. When I went out for the evening, I wanted to make sure I looked visibly disabled. Back at home I always tried to cover up my leg, but here, if people could see my leg, I would be welcomed into every conversation, asked to dance, and be automatically accepted by every other disabled person there.

Because losing a limb happens to people in random ways, this was the most diverse group of people you'd ever find. There were young kids, older people, Vietnam vets, people in wheelchairs, people on crutches, people missing arms, and blind people. People came from the deep South, the Northeast, and the far West. There were blue collar workers drinking with Ph.D.'s. The great thing was this outpouring of love that you got by being disabled. You were instantly accepted. I had never experienced anything like it.

Back at home, my mother had started dating Sidney Schwimmer, a Jewish man of Eastern European descent with a very large family in San Diego and in Chicago. They moved in together, which meant he was living with me, too. Both my mother and Sidney were thrilled about my skiing achievements.

After doing well at my first national championships, I saw that I could aim for a spot on the US Team for the 1984 Paralympics in Innsbruck, Austria. But I knew I needed a coach and access to skiing more than weekends.

On the back of the book, *How the Racers Ski*, I saw that the author was the headmaster of a high school for ski racers in Vermont. I was amazed that such a thing could exist. I called and asked them to send more information.

I remember sitting on my bed with my brother looking at the brochures for Burke Mountain Academy: kids training in obstacle courses in fall, skiing together in winter, and studying together in log cabins near the ski area. Instead of living in San Diego and struggling to get on snow two days a week, I could live on a mountain and have the best coaches in the nation! The fact that no other amputees were in the pictures did not slow me down. But the price tag did: $8,400 for tuition might as well have been a million in my family.

"This is impossible," I said to my brother. "So I might as well get started." If I failed, I'd be no worse off . . . still sitting on my bed. I had nothing to lose, so I might as well try.

I applied to Burke Mountain Academy and was accepted as a student. For three months I searched for grants, scholarships, and sponsors, to no avail. The school had agreed to give me a partial scholarship and the headmaster knew I was trying to raise the rest. I will never forget the moment when I told the headmaster I couldn't afford the tuition and I had failed to find sponsors.

He said, "Come anyway."

I knew this opportunity would change my life. Not, however, in the ways I expected.

Just before I left for Vermont, my mother married Sidney Schwimmer in a small ceremony with friends and family in our backyard. As the last child leaving home, I was glad that she wouldn't be alone.

On my first day at Burke Mountain Academy, I broke my

leg—my real leg—while playing on a skateboard. As the only kid with one leg, I had so badly wanted to show them I could run obstacle courses, jump rope, and play soccer. Instead, walking on crutches with my artificial leg I could barely get from my room to dinner without tripping on stones on the path. Nothing real was touching the ground. Being thoroughly inept among a crowd of super athletes hurt more than my injuries. At night, I cried into my pillow to keep my roommate from hearing.

When the doctor cut off my cast after six weeks, my luck did not turn. Less than a week out of my cast, my artificial leg broke in half. Then, for three weeks my prosthesis roamed around the country lost in the U.S. Postal Service system.

I kept waiting for someone to say to me, "Okay, you have no money and you've busted up your legs. It's time for you to go." I thought my mother would call and tell me to come home immediately. I kept waiting to be shown the door. But it never happened.

If none of the adults thought I had to go, I certainly wasn't going to bring up the idea. I had fought and scraped to get where I was. Some outside force or external circumstance might stop me, but I would not stop myself.

I spent the extra time while I was injured with Burke's fund-raiser, hunting for grants to defray my tuition costs and training expenses. A lucky break came through in early January of 1982, when I received a response by phone.

"This is Ben Finley," he said, in a voice bubbling with laughter. "I am the president of the National Brotherhood of Skiers." It was one of the many organizations I had contacted for help. "We sponsor promising young black skiers," he said. "That sounds like you."

"Well, thanks. I could sure use some help," I said in shock. My hard work had paid off!

"Can we interest you in a trip to Park City, Utah? We're having a meeting out here and I'd like to present you to the board of directors. I think you can get some funding support out of this."

The opening ceremony for the NBS Summit convention at Park City, Utah, was held at the foot of the mountain. Over four hundred of the convention participants were gathered on the patio at the edge of the lodge and shops. The mountain peaks, covered with snow, fir trees, and gently curving ski trails, provided an otherworldly backdrop for the podium.

Speakers included African-American movie stars, politicians, and club officials. They told inspirational and humorous stories to kick off the largest ski convention in the country. How can it be that the largest ski convention in the United States each year is comprised of African Americans? Why do thousands of NBS members drop what they are doing to attend this outrageous week of skiing and celebrating?

NBS members are not into segregation or isolation. They probably didn't make their money or learn how to ski without learning to "hang with the white folks." Most NBS members spend most of the year completely surrounded by white people, except for this one week of the year when the tables are turned and whites are in the minority.

Furthermore, this group has a lot more in common than the color of their skin—and a lot more to celebrate. Typically, Summit attendees are successful and wealthy or they couldn't afford to be at the week-long ski convention. Most are well educated and have diverse interests, of which skiing is only one. None of them hindered by the myths like, "black people can't ski," or "black people don't like cold weather." This is not just any group of black people, it is a group of champions. As much as my disabled ski groups helped me enjoy being handicapped, the Brotherhood of Skiers gave me the opportunity to grow into my identity as an African American.

The NBS helped me survive at Burke. The NBS made it possible for me to enter ski races with the other Burkies by paying my race fees and providing spending money for meals and lodging as we traveled across the Northeast. In addition, NBS found more ski clothes for me and paid thousands of dollars toward my tuition at Burke. A personal touch came when Gertrude, an NBS member from Boston, was the only person in attendance for me at my high school graduation because my mother couldn't afford to come.

I wish I had known Vonetta Flowers' story back then. If I had been praying, I might not have felt like I had to carry everything on my shoulders. Competition is stressful, but in an expensive winter sport where the people don't look like you, there are additional pressures. Vonetta excelled by turning over the stress to God in prayer and focusing her energy on doing her best. I did it the hard way, with a lot less joy.

Libby Pataki

During the time when her husband, George, was running for governor of New York, Libby Pataki experienced some of the most intense public speaking demands she'd ever had to face. Due to scheduling conflicts of the campaign, there were many times when she was called upon to stand in for her husband.

The first time she had to speak in public for her husband, Libby was terrified. Her body started to shake and she gripped the podium for support. She thought to herself, "Oh my gosh, I'll never be as good as George. I'll never be able to do this." Somehow, when it was over, she felt, "That wasn't so bad, I can do that." Each time, however, the tension mounted beforehand and her body shook.

Someone suggested that before stepping up to the dais she should take three breaths and pray, "Be still and know that I am God."*

"Be still . . . be still . . . be still," she'd repeat to herself over and

---

* Psalm 46:10 KJV.

over. The shaking would slow and finally she'd begin to feel a calmness come over her. All she had to do was ask for help.

But she began to notice that when she was making speeches she was only praying be still, be still when she needed help. Libby realized that it is also important to say thank you. So she began to pray for help at the beginning of a speech and then she'd say a prayer of thanks when she got down from the podium.

That was a long time ago. Libby Pataki has evolved into a seasoned and confident speaker, making speeches all over the country. She shares how her reliance on God and His miraculous gift of nature has helped her deal with the often stressful and chaotic world of politics.

As first lady of New York State, you have to be ready for anything: intense media scrutiny and harsh criticism become commonplace. Because my life has been such a rollercoaster, when I've been the most afraid I've learned that what I needed to do most was just step back and say, "I need help."

We live in a wonderful community in Garrison, New York, surrounded by woods. My routine—on the days that I can—is to get up very, very early, around 6:00 a.m. and walk in the hills. It reminds me to "Be still and know that I am God."

That's where I feel that the most. I walk to be out in the woods and get myself in the right frame of mind, to just be peaceful.

I like to walk for about an hour, so that's why I have to do it early, before the day starts. In essence, I feel like, for an hour, I can literally leave things behind. I can walk to the top of the hill. I can just breathe and listen. I hear birds. I hear the wind. I look up and it is so pretty sometimes. Even when it is not pretty, I am in a quiet place, just where I want to be.

It isn't forced. I don't necessarily say, "Today I am going to walk and pray." Prayer is tied into the physical, mental, and spiritual. It's all of those things. You have the endorphins from walking up the hill. You're physically a little relaxed, and winding down from getting your heart going. Prayer is for good health as well.

To listen to God, you have to be someplace quiet. You have to turn off the cell phone and the BlackBerry. You have to hear what is coming back. If you are surrounded by people handing you phones, you can't hear what God is saying.

Listening to God is not like hearing voices. What happens to me is that I get into a frame of mind where a tranquility comes over me that enables me to go back down the hill and not be swallowed by the things that are thrown at me, to not be overwhelmed by what's waiting for me.

It's a feeling of serenity. It's not specific words. It's not as though God tells me, "At 9:30 this particular issue will come up and this is what I want you to say." God isn't saying "do this or do that." I have to make my own decisions. But He is putting me into a frame of mind where things are not as overwhelming, and I am better able to cope. I think God wants me to help myself.

By spending the time listening on the top of the hill, I feel like I form a link with God that stays with me all day. It isn't that I hear everything I need on the mountain top, but I am better able to listen as I go through my day. I am in a more peaceful place to deal with everything.

Have you ever been around people who have a serenity about them? Things just don't bother them so much. With that serenity, I can respond from a place of listening rather than the way people typically seem to talk over each other all the time.

Upon becoming first lady, I was surprised to discover that New York was the only state in the US that did not host a prayer breakfast in conjunction with the National Day of Prayer. My husband and I initiated the tradition and have celebrated the day as a special event for the twelve years he has served as governor.

When I look back on all the prayer breakfasts, I really think it has helped my husband. In the very beginning when I said I wanted to have one, all of the staff said, "Oh no! One more thing we have to do!" They saw it as a chore because it took a lot of work to put a prayer breakfast together. There was so much to do. But the prayer breakfast always refreshed him. I think it gave him a different perspective. When you go to a prayer breakfast, you have different speakers and people of different denominations. You are getting extra strength from other worlds: the private sector world; people who are suffering; people in the media.

In the past, we've had astronauts speak, Yankees team managers, even Kathy Lee Gifford. It gives George an opportunity to brush up against people with different experiences and draw strength from them.

This year we had a Jewish rabbi, a Muslim Imam, and a Baptist minister all speak at the same breakfast. There were blacks and whites; men and women; many religions together. It wasn't like your traditional worship service. It's important to get the perspective of other people. The prayer breakfast does that in an important way.

Down by the Riverside

Under a thick covering of pine trees that shut out the bright summer sunshine, I sat down on a boulder next to a shallow stream. It was dark, cool, and damp. I felt a sense of peace and rest, hypnotized by the song of the water. I spent many hours there that summer.

Within twenty-four hours after graduating from Burke Mountain Academy, I was riding on a bus up to Mt. Hood, Oregon, to live and work on a glacier for the summer. Through contacts at Burke, I had located Mike Annette's summer ski training program and signed up for it. I had applied for all kinds of jobs in the ski lodge and been accepted as a cashier in the gift shop.

My year at Burke had been a tough one. I was as far away from home as was possible while still in the USA. I broke my real leg then my artificial leg. I looked for sponsors and applied to colleges at the same time I lived in constant fear of running out of money. I did not fit in with the other kids at Burke—some even told me they hated me. All year I had struggled.

But this summer I could relax a little. Things were looking up. I was accepted to Harvard University for fall. I was sponsored by the National Brotherhood of Skiers. Then, on my first day at summer ski camp headquarters, I ran into Cathy Gentile, the young woman who had taken me to my first national championships. She had arrived with the same idea—to train for the summer.

It was my lucky day. We were the only two amputee skiers living on Mt. Hood that summer, we knew each other, and we arrived on the same day! We agreed to share an apartment for the summer.

No parents, no school, no kids to feel left out from. I didn't have a car, but I could walk from end to end of the small town in a few minutes or catch the shuttle up to the lodge at the top of the mountain.

Every morning on weekdays, I trained with the race camp from 8:00 a.m. until noon. The glacier was on a craggy mountain peak with volcanic rocks and snowy crevasses. Most days, you could see for hundreds of miles into the valley below us. There was no training in the afternoon because the hot summer sun makes the snow too slushy to ski on.

After training, I usually went down to the gift shop, changed into street clothes, and worked for the afternoon until the store closed. Weekends, the busiest time with tourists, I worked all day long both days.

Carol Haughk, the store manager, wanted to support my bid for the Olympics and gave me the perfect schedule to work around my ski training. Almost all the young people who worked in the ski lodge over the summer wanted a schedule that worked around the limited morning ski hours. Carol could not have run her business if she let everyone work those hours. That she maximized my ski time was a tremendous gift.

It was hard work, but not stressful in the way so much of my life had been. I felt peaceful living close to nature up on that mountain. I had no television, movie theater, or Internet access. I read works by Herman Hesse and Ayn Rand, and the *Tao Te Ching*. I picked huckleberries that grew wild in the woods. We made pies and shakes, and ate berries with ice cream. Mostly, I rested inside myself.

One day, I was riding on the chairlift with a tourist who told me he was reading a book on self-hypnosis. "How does that work?" I asked. He described it to me in brief and I decided to try it for myself.

The next day, before race camp training, I sat still, closed my eyes, and imagined walking down a flight of fifty stairs, counting each one. At the bottom I saw two doors. I entered the first door and, as he suggested, imagined myself in a wonderful place. For me it was a future where I was a wealthy, jet setting, grown up, traveling to exciting places and meeting interesting people.

Behind the second door, I saw my inner self. I told her that we were going to training in a few minutes. I asked her to listen carefully to the coaches, make each training run count, and let my body learn the new moves. She agreed with me to focus on the training and repeated back everything I had asked her to do. I opened my eyes and went to camp.

Forgetting all about the silly self-hypnosis game, I threw myself into the day's race course. Up and down the hill I went, listening to my coach, trying harder each time. At the end of the day, I thought, "Wow, what a great day. I was so focused. Every run seemed to provide a wealth of learning. My body took on new skills with ease." Then it hit me. Everything I suggested to myself in the meditation was there for me in training. It worked!

After that, I used this mental focus technique for everything: for training, for races, for exams in college. As an adult I used this focus technique for speeches and even to prepare for childbirth. I never read any books on it myself, but I practiced with it and got better and better. When you think about it, it is just common sense: if you relax deeply and ask your innermost self to help you with something, you are more likely to be able to do it than if you don't.

Without that slowed-down summer on a glacier (and another summer on the glacier the following year), I don't know whether I would have learned to close my eyes and go deep inside myself. I don't know if I would have found the strength to climb the mountains in my life.

Perhaps the reason I was drawn to skiing in the first place was the way that mountains strengthened me. The crisp, thin air forced me to breathe more deeply and washed clean my lungs and bloodstream. The trees and rocks seemed to pour out a love and support for me that didn't ask anything in return. The breathtaking, dramatic glacier scenery humbled me, inspired me, and brought joy into my heart. But most of all, I enjoyed the quiet time spent sitting beside the cool stream behind my house and letting the water wash away my cares. On Mt. Hood, I was restored.

Libby Pataki talked about being in nature. In future chapters, Christine Todd Whitman, Kelly Hoke, and others talk about the powerful effect of praying in nature. It is almost as if you can't help but pray when surrounded by trees, flowers, and mountains.

Ann Marie Maloney also suggests that if you aren't ready to start praying, try just sitting still and being quiet. When I slowed down and cut out the chatter of TV, computers, phones, and non-stop activity, I made space to begin hearing God and open the door to a relationship with Him. I didn't know it at the time, but the habit of "self-hypnosis" that I took with me off the mountain would be the way that God was finally able to get through to me.

Nadia Comaneci

In 1976, at the Olympic Games in Montreal, Canada, the world was collectively fascinated with the story of Nadia Comaneci. She was the pint-sized Romanian girl with the signature pony tail who won five gold medals and scored the first perfect ten in the history of gymnastics. She captivated us all with a strength and style that revolutionized her sport.

But back at home, life was not easy for Nadia and her family under the oppressive Romanian government. The country's dictator, President Nicolae Ceausescu and his wife, Elana, took much of the food the country produced and sold it overseas to buy luxuries for themselves. At one point, many Romanians worked seven days a week and were rationed to only two pounds of meat per month.

In 1989, Nadia and six others took the chance of their lives and made a desperate attempt to defect from their native Romania. Escaping into pitch black darkness, Nadia and her companions fled into a bone chillingly cold winter night with temperatures well below-zero. Each one touched the shoulders of the next to ensure their little group stayed together—using flashlights would attract the guards and mean certain death.

She would later write in her book, *Letters to a Young Gymnast,** that she always prayed. "I prayed my parents would be well, for I left them out of my scheme, and that my brother would be untouched. I prayed that I would be able to move one foot in front of the other."

After an excruciatingly long night of walking, falling through ice into frigid water, they trudged onward and crossed the Hungarian border. A friend drove them to the Austrian border where they spent the next night climbing barbed wire fences. A bloodied, but determined, Nadia showed up at the US embassy and was quickly offered asylum.

Nadia's story would not be possible without prayer and determination.

After retiring from gymnastics, I worked for many years in a government job, supervising athletic facilities. I was not only trying to support myself but also help my brother, his wife, and my parents, too. I barely made enough money for heat or food to eat.

My every move and every word in public were under surveillance. I wasn't even allowed to travel with the national gymnastics team on which I became so well known throughout the world, because the government feared I would defect as my coaches, Bela and Marta Karolyis, had already done in 1981. I was essentially a prisoner and a puppet.

---

* Letters to a Young Gymnast (the Art of Mentoring) *by Nadia Comaneci. New York: Perseus Books, 2004. Used with permission.*

I wrote about my feelings in my book, *Letters to a Young Gymnast:*

> "Do you understand, dear friend, how desperate a
> person must be to attempt defection? I had to
> weigh the value of seeking a better life against the
> probability of my imprisonment or death if I failed
> in the effort.
> "There are moments in life when you lose your edge,
> so to speak. Even though there's a small voice
> inside you that is desperately trying to shake you
> out of the haze, it is hard to hear it.
> "Try always to listen to that voice because it speaks
> the truth, even when you don't want to hear what
> it is saying."

I don't like to talk about that time too much, the defection. It was scary and a lot of people who tried didn't make it. I am sure most people think that once I defected all of my problems were finally over. But it took years for me to remove the bars inside my head and learn to feel and be free.

At times, I trusted the wrong people. I sometimes said the wrong things to the press. After being in the USA for a while, I rekindled my friendship with US gymnast Bart Conner. Bart had won two medals in gymnastics at the 1984 Olympics, in Los Angeles. Our relationship eventually blossomed into love and marriage.

Bart is my best friend and a wonderful husband. He is very kind and tender. We've been married for more than ten years, but sometimes I feel like we are still newlyweds. Today we live with our son, Dylan, in Norman, Oklahoma, and supervise a gymnastics training center.

I don't talk much about it, but my relationship with God is an important part of my life. I was not allowed to talk about religion while growing up because it was prohibited at that particular time, when Romania was a communist country. But despite the risks, I grew up in a family that prayed every night.

We grew up with both our grandmothers telling us that we have to kneel down every night to say the Lord's Prayer. Even though we could get into trouble, my family went to church anyway. Of course, I went with my family because I wanted to go to church. For people who had a name in that country, actors or athletes, it was better to not be caught in that situation. I went, but I always wore something on my head and nobody knew who I was. We were never punished because we didn't get caught!

I've prayed all my life. I prayed when I was competing. I pray when I fly, I pray when I travel, and I pray when I do a press conference. I pray all the time, but I don't make the sign of a cross in front of everybody, because that's not me. For me, praying is very private.

I think some people externalize it and they like to preach about it. They like to be seen praying. I believe prayer is private and personal. I don't even like to talk to Bart about it. He sees me just kneel down wherever I am and he doesn't ask about it.

Much of my life I succeeded in things that I tried to accomplish, so I believe prayer made me stronger. That strength comes from the family that I grew up in. We all had faith. They made me believe that all things are possible if you go in the right direction, use your instinct, and rely on what you know. Prayer makes you stronger, but it also makes you believe that whatever you do, it will work.

Our prayers are not always answered in the way we think

they should be. If something doesn't happen the way you want it to, you should wait and say "Well, maybe this isn't the time when this is supposed to happen and it will happen later." Keep your thoughts positive. You should never be upset about God and your prayers.

My prayers have remained the same. I still pray in Romanian. I don't even know if I could find the words in English. I stick with what I learned thirty years ago. I add new names of people who I want to pray for. I don't think prayer needs to be complex: "Help me God." It's not that complicated.

You have to trust God. You can't be angry. I believe what goes around, comes around. You reap what you sow. How you are, is what you get back.

Paralympic Silver Medalist

Over five hundred athletes from twenty-two countries gathered in January at Innsbruck, Austria, for the 1984 Paralympic Games. There were banners, flags and camera crews. I was so excited to have my team jacket and to be representing my country. As the third-ranked amputee woman in the US, I had only just made the cut (they only took three, one-legged women). But I was just happy to be there. After breaking my legs in high school and taking a leave of absence from Harvard to train, my dream to be a member of the US Disabled Ski Team was a reality at last!

My mother and my stepfather, Sidney, came to watch, along with my sister, April, and my brother, Wayne. Thirty-three members of the NBS came to cheer for me. When my teammates saw this large group of African Americans on the hill in Europe cheering for me, they said, "Bonnie, you have a really big family!"

"Yes, I do!" was my response.

My mother had never seen me race before. Obviously, ski races weren't held in San Diego. With three kids in college, she could not afford to fly across the country to watch me race.

But there I was, with all the world's eyes upon me. I went down the course for the first run of the slalom race. Slalom is the race with very tight turns around the red and blue poles. When I reached the bottom and the times were posted, I was in first place! As other skiers finished, I remained in the lead. What a stunning upset! No one expected me to beat my teammates, never mind everyone else in the world!

All my hard work paid off: training with two-legged champions at Burke, spending two summers on a glacier, and hard physical training in the fall. I was stronger and had more hours on snow this year than the other skiers. My mother went berserk! She jumped up and down screaming.

She couldn't stand the excitement—and the suspense. To win the gold medal, I had to complete a second run. While waiting for the second run, her nerves were frayed. I left to find a quiet place to focus my mind for the second run.

In ski races, you never ski the same course twice. I inspected the new course and then went back to the top of the course to await my turn. As I sat in the snow near the start area, I heard that the women ahead of me were crashing on a dangerous, icy spot in the course.

I stood in the start gate while the race official counted down, "Five! . . . Four! . . . Three! . . . Two! . . . One!" I left the start, breaking the timing wand. I began to turn tightly, hitting the blue and red poles with my outriggers. I got to where I could see the finish line and thought, "I've made it! I'm past the ice!" That's when I hit it. I tried to dig in with my ski and hold my edge, but I couldn't. Wham! I was on my rear end in the snow.

Can you imagine how it feels to be number one in the world one minute, and the next minute sitting on your tush in the snow? I wanted to crawl away and not have to face my mother, my teammates, my sponsors, and friends.

All those thoughts went through my head in a split second. Then my reflexes took over. Gathering my outriggers, I stood up and finished the race. When the dust cleared and times were in, my time was still in third place. All the top women took the tightest line, hit the ice, fell and then finished. That night, I stood on the winner's podium with the US flag waving behind me, my mother sobbing in the snow as they hung the bronze medal around my neck and gave me a bouquet of flowers.

The next day, I again placed third in the Giant Slalom—a similar race with wider turns. Finally, I placed seventh in the downhill race, the race where you wear a helmet and ski almost straight down the mountain on one leg at speeds over sixty miles per hour!

At the final medals ceremony, I was awarded the silver medal for overall performance as the second fastest woman in the world on one leg! It was many years later that I would find out I was, in fact, the first African American to win medals in any Winter Olympics or Paralympics.

However, I wouldn't have won the overall medal if I hadn't finished that first slalom race. I thought about how I had been the leader in the first run. I was arguably the best slalom skier in the world. The Austrian woman who won the gold in that race had also fallen and gotten up in the second run. I realized that I was likely skiing faster than her until

I fell. Then it hit me! She didn't beat me by skiing faster. She beat me by getting up faster! Everyone fell. The winners were those who got up and finished. But the gold medal winner was the one who got up the fastest.

The reason my family could afford to go on a trip to Europe to watch me race was that Paul had died about ten months before the Paralympics. I don't remember it well; I was traveling and training. My mother had already married Sidney. Paul left $1,000 to each of us kids, plus more cash and a trust fund for my mother. Everyone opted to use the inherited money to come and support me in Austria.

When my stepfather died, I began to remember a little bit about the games he played with me alone in my bedroom as a child. I had suppressed the memories completely for so many years. It is funny how it comes back, though. I didn't wake up one day, remember it, become shocked and begin crying. You can't be shocked, because you always knew. It feels more like a small side road that was always there, but you haven't walked down it for years.

The first time or two a memory surfaced, I just pushed the thought away, thinking, "Oh, that old memory." Then one day I realized, though, I always knew, I had never talked about it to anyone.

It is well documented in books on the subject that many people find the memories resurface after the death of the perpetrator. The next time I saw my mother, I told her about the memories.

"What does it matter?" she asked. "He's dead. It's over. Get on with your life. The same thing happened to me and I put it behind me. You should, too."

It sounded like good advice. I thought people who

wallowed in their history were weak and just making excuses to avoid doing the hard work of living in the present.

Within a week after returning to the US from the Paralympics in Innsbruck, Austria, classes resumed at Harvard for the spring term. I found myself lost and disoriented, trying to shift gears from the intensity of years of skiing into the intensity of mental competitiveness. Even wearing normal clothing every day, instead of ski clothes, felt alien. It took time to adjust—time and extra tutoring on my writing.

Nadia Comaneci faced many difficulties during and after her Olympic wins. Prayer gave her the courage to make a change in her life and escape. Prayer helped her through the transformation to live in freedom and find love. But I was trying do everything myself, without God's help, so I continued to live in fear and stuff down my emotions.

For example, when I had to walk all over the campus at Harvard to get to classes and libraries, sometimes my leg would get sore. Rather than ask for help, I just kept going, even to the point where my stump would turn into sore, raw meat inside my prosthesis. In a sense, I was my own dictator, pushing myself to excel and too afraid to lean on others, really enjoy myself, or express my feelings.

Amy Domini

La Oroya is a small village in Peru at 14,000 feet in the mountains. Virtually all of its four-hundred villagers work for Doe Run, a privately-owned American company.

The children in the town—and for about twenty kilometers in any direction—test at four-hundred times average positive for lead in their bloodstreams, according to Oxfam America, a nonprofit that tries to find lasting solutions to poverty and hunger. The children are sick, and the primary reason is became they are living in the gray shadow of Doe Run's lead smelter.

Lead has a permanent, long-term detrimental impact on human health, the most common of which is reducing one's IQ. The thing about lead poisoning is that the children don't just die. They smile a little longer than most children smile. They are slower. This is a problem that takes a hundred years to solve and it has been going on for fifty years—long before Doe Run acquired the facility. Domini met with the US embassy in Lima, Peru to express her dismay that Americans could stand by and let this happen.

She says she thought they were more interested in talking about fighting the drug war. But she wasn't.

Domini Social Investments, where Amy serves as CEO, was founded to address situations like this. The company's first mutual fund was launched in 1991. The company now invests funds totaling almost $2 billion for a wide range of individuals and institutions who wish to use their investments to build a better world.

Because her company manages a significant amount of dollars, Amy and her colleagues can get meetings with top CEOs from around the globe. Their clout allows them to pull together shareholder groups to request the publication of more information about a company's impact on the planet and its people. *Time* magazine named Amy Domini one of the hundred most influential people in the world because Amy has built up this clout and used it to make a difference, paving the way for a $30 billion dollar industry of social investment funds.

Since Doe Run is a private company, Domini's firm can't buy their stock, and that makes the situation hard to influence. The owner of Doe Run is Ira Rennert, best known for having the biggest house in America, a 100,000 sq. ft. mansion in South Hampton. However, Domini does own Johnson Controls stock, an important customer of Doe Run, and that is where they turned to get access. Johnson Controls, which purchases lead from Doe Run for use in car batteries, has a good corporate social responsibility profile, and was willing to talk. Eventually, Domini was able to use its leverage with Johnson Controls to bring Doe Run to the table.

Explains Domini, "In effect, we told them: 'Doe Run owns the smelter, but it is your responsibility. You are their biggest customer. You have some power with them. Get them to the table.'" Doe Run came to a meeting with Domini's team and a group of religious investors affiliated with the Interfaith Center on Corporate Responsibility.

The company made its case, explaining what they have done in the community, and what they planned to do. Doe Run heard the concerns of shareholders who are willing to use their assets to fight for the health of La Oroya's children.

National Public Radio ran a show in February 2007 that focused on the situation in La Oroya. They found that most people there are afraid to talk to outsiders. They have so little that they cannot lose more, and they fear that outsiders will close the factory and cost them their jobs.

Domini says this is an ongoing story and she doesn't know how it will end. But, she points out that twenty-five years ago the concept that finance might have human implications was off the table. But fast forward to 2006, and over six-thousand corporations around the world published a corporate social impact report of some sort or other. It is now generally accepted that corporations do have an impact on the people and ecology of the planet. Today, looking at these impacts is a legitimate investment criteria, just like portfolio turnover or return on assets.

"If we want to make the world safe," Domini says, "we need to start with the big, powerful engines that are available. The most powerful of these engines are fueled by capital, and this capital is widely held by ordinary people like you and me in the form of stocks and bonds, in mutual funds. It is up to us to steer these engines into the future. I am proud of the progress we have made in making finance part of the answer."

My father once told me that there was no life after death. He said, "If there was life after death, I would know," because as a young man he had hidden in mass graves for six weeks in Italy, waiting for the allied forces to arrive.

My mother was from a well-to-do family and lived a sheltered life in lower Manhattan. Her father worked in the financial industry. My parents met when my mother went to Italy after World War II to volunteer in an orphanage. After they married, she raised me as a Congregationalist, probably for convenience, because it was the local church.

My work allows me to travel around the world. I attend services in many countries, cultures, and religions. I have been in Panama seven times this year. I go to the Catholic church there, even though I can't understand a word! I still get a lot out of it. When I go to church in Latin America or in Europe, there are babies everywhere and lots of images of women. I find the New England Protestant settings where I grew up so dismally masculine in comparison . . . needlessly so. Lately, I have been feeling that I need to find a different worship setting. I haven't found that perfect setting that gives me the community side of prayer.

I do not have a time when I take out certain instruments and recite long prayers, but there are certain times that I always pray. For example, when someone is leaving and won't be back for a long time. Also, I always pray last thing before I go to sleep. Sometimes I get on my knees. Mostly, I don't.

Usually, it is part of my unwinding from the day. I confess it could be while I am in bed, getting ready to go to sleep or sometimes even while I am brushing my teeth!

I am very aware that often when I go to sleep problems solve themselves. Answers come to me, so I want to have my head ready for that. Practically always, I have some terrible stress in my life, like the time when there was an audit at the same time the board meeting was coming up. Why did they have to do it right then? But there is always something.

When you are running a business with almost two billion dollars of other people's money, there is always some stress from that. The challenge of business is that you must take risks.

Also, I have two sons, both on a very slow, leisurely path through college. I find that with prayer I can wipe all those things out of my mind and revert to a core Amy. I use prayer to get to that place where problems can solve themselves overnight.

I start with the Lord's Prayer. Then I look at the key things on my mind that day. In a way, it is like cataloging everything or putting it up on a wall, organizing things. There may be a friend who lost someone close to them. There is always some issue with my children. Once these things are all there on the shelf, I will turn to the thing I want to dream about, the thing I want to solve. I definitely ask God to work with me in areas where I feel I am too edgy. I ask for patience, I ask for perspective. I focus on things I think I can solve overnight with prayer.

Another time I pray is when I am going into a stressful situation. I realized four or five years ago that I could put myself into "the zone" by praying, and actually lower my heart rate. If I know I am going into a setting where I might get very emotional or if I just want to stay very focused, I use prayer as a calming influence. Part of it is very centering and the other part is giving myself over.

I have this vision of being held in these hands. I feel I am just being placed there—it isn't about me getting myself there. This really helps in those places where I don't need to march into the room and take over. No, I am just being delivered into this setting as the messenger for you. Having this vision of being placed in the room . . . it is gentle and comforting. If I didn't take the time to quiet down and remember that before I went in I probably would have a harder time. There is a stripping of the ego. I don't know if I would say I am doing God's work. I just feel that I am gently and safely placed in certain positions.

Summer on Wall Street

BONNIE'S STORY

It was two o'clock in the morning. I was so tired I could barely keep my eyes open, but I felt great. It was the first week of my internship at Morgan Stanley, an investment banking firm I was placed in by Sponsors for Educational Opportunity (SEO), a group that brought minorities into Wall Street jobs.

I had been asked to work late in order to prepare a presentation for an early morning meeting. Taking numbers from the market close, we created pages and pages, analyzing the financial position of a prospective client, suggesting some transactions to enhance their finances. By morning, we had published a custom-made book of advice with up-to-the-minute, accurate information.

Although I only did the grunt work of arranging, checking, and rechecking the calculations, I was thrilled and proud. Columns on the page were headed "mm" for millions as though it were Monopoly money. I was in awe of the partners, in their expensive suits, and the understated luxury of the office furniture, rugs, and art. I couldn't believe I was really in the inner sanctum of power.

Since we stayed so late at work, they let us order dinner from a fancy restaurant that delivered to the office . . . and not just pizza or sandwiches. I was given a voucher for a sleek, Lincoln Town Car to take me safely home through the city streets in the wee morning hours . . . not a taxi. I felt important. As a teacher, my mother never got treated this way.

As the summer continued, I came to see that everyone there was smart and talented, whether they worked copy machines or led the team. Only people willing to work long hours on short notice could survive. Dinner ordered in and a sedan ride home soon became routine. Because of the crazy hours, most people in investment banking lost all their friends in the outside world. After canceling plans at the last minute too many times, people stop inviting you.

Despite the hard work, or perhaps because of it, I loved the atmosphere. After Olympic training and studying at Harvard, I was used to total dedication in pursuit of excellence. It felt comfortable.

I also loved the money. My summer intern salary was a small fortune to me. I could see myself there in the future making millions. For the little girl who spent her whole life being afraid of running out of money, Wall Street looked like paradise. I thought all my problems in life would be over if I could just earn enough money to feel safe and secure. At this point in my life, I still did not put any faith in God.

One Friday, my boss asked me to work all weekend, helping a group of partners put the final touches on a bid to buy Conrail. I was just there to get coffee, faxes, and anything else they needed, but I was ecstatic.

There was a woman partner who asked me to get a blue folder off her desk. As I strode purposefully down the plush corridor to her corner office, I was imagining being her someday. I stepped into "my" office and scanned "my" breathtaking view of Manhattan.

Just as I reached for the blue file on her desk, something out of place caught my eye. It was a crude crayon drawing of two stick figures, one big and one small. Under the bigger person was written, "MOM aT WoRk." The smaller figure was shedding a big tear over the words, "ME At hOmE."

The bubble containing my perfect future burst. Here she was still at work all weekend. How could she keep that picture on her desk? I began to wonder about the personal price tag for all this. Maybe I shouldn't have a family, I thought. I still wanted the money, power, and security, but I began to look more closely at the lifestyle it required. Despite the pros and cons, by the end of the summer I was ready to sign up for a job after college. I was willing to believe in money more than anything else.

I did not know at the time that I didn't have to sacrifice my values or my life to work on Wall Street. I didn't have spiritual role models on Wall Street. It was five years after my internship that Amy Domini started her fund for social investments. I didn't know that I could work on Wall Street and be a change for the better in the world at the same time.

Today I know a number of women who are leaders in the New York financial world who pray before meetings, pray about handling the difficult people issues at work, and pray about their career decisions. One such woman is Carla Harris, a managing director at Morgan Stanley, the same firm where I was an intern. A powerful dealmaker and one of the firm's most senior women, she also sings gospel music at Carnegie Hall as part of a major annual fundraiser for schools in Harlem. Similarly, Westina Matthews, who I write about in a later chapter, is a Merrill Lynch senior executive completing a program for spiritual directors in her "spare" time. If I had looked up to people like Carla Harris, Westina Matthews and Amy Domini, I would have thought about a career on Wall Street in an entirely different way, bringing the best of both worlds together.

Back at college for my senior year, my life returned to the usual pressures. I used up my summer earnings paying off the portion of my tuition my mother was responsible for and my bookstore credit account. I still had to bartend to make money for my day-to-day expenses. My studies were intense. I wrote a thesis analyzing Japanese financial markets, took my honors exams, and finished *magna cum laude*.

I applied for several fellowships, including the prestigious Rhodes Scholarship.

I was more surprised than anyone when I won. The Rhodes Scholarship provided two years of free study at Oxford University in England, plus a travel budget. Making money on Wall Street would have to wait until after I saw the world.

PART III

FROM MARRIAGE TO POLITICS: POWERFUL RELATIONSHIPS

Marilyn McCoo

Marilyn, meet my friend Billy."

Marilyn McCoo was the tall, statuesque, sultry-voiced singer who would later become the accomplished platinum album singer and actress, probably best known as a member of the 5th Dimension singing group alongside the charming and handsome Billy Davis, Jr.

Lamonte McLemore introduced them because they both loved singing. They seemed to be opposites in every other way. Marilyn was a college graduate and the daughter of two doctors. Billy had dropped out of high school and survived on street smarts.

Marilyn knew Lamonte from singing with him in a group called the "HiFis." She had stopped by his house one Saturday night just to hang out. Billy had left St. Louis and was staying with Lamonte in Los Angeles in hopes of making it big in the music business. "Billy can really sing," Lamonte told Marilyn. "He's out here trying to get a deal with Motown." Motown had a West Coast office for auditions.

Billy flashed his thousand-watt smile and his laugh filled the room. His hair had been "processed" real straight and slick like the popular singers of the day. Billy was funny and a life-of-the-party type. He was passionate about music and talked with Marilyn for a couple of hours that night.

Some weeks later, Lamonte suggested that they form a new singing group for something to do while waiting for Motown to give them each a contract. He approached Billy first.

"That sounds like fun," Billy said. "But just so you know, I'm not giving up on my solo career."

When he approached Marilyn she was more dubious.

"You remember how nobody was serious about it when we were doing the Hi-Fis," she reminded him. "I've had enough of picking up people from their girlfriend's house and starting rehearsals two hours late."

Lamonte handed the phone to Billy. "No, this will be different," Billy said. "First of all, we're talking about doing this as a hobby—something to pass the time until our solo careers get going. And I think we are all professional enough to show up on time for practice. We'll rehearse after you get off work."

Billy won over Marilyn. They recruited two more people, Florence LaRue and Ronald Townson, forming the group that would eventually become famous as the 5th Dimension, winning six GRAMMY Awards and cutting fourteen gold records, including songs like "Up, Up and Away," "Aquarius," and "One Less Bell to Answer."

After leaving the 5th Dimension, Marilyn and Billy opted to sing duets so that solo careers would not pull apart their relationship. Their duo hits included, "You Don't Have to Be a Star," which earned them yet another GRAMMY.

Today, after more than thirty years of marriage in the pressure cooker of the music industry, prayer is the rock on which they stand, as individuals and as a couple.

(adapted from the book *Up, Up, and Away**, *by Marilyn and Billy*)

Even though we are so excited about my husband's twenty years of sobriety and how he overcame his struggles with alcohol, Billy had never shared his alcoholism story at the lunches and events at which we give speeches. Then, one day it changed.

We were in the hotel room, getting ready to go downstairs to give a speech in about an hour. I said to Billy, "You never talk about your struggle with alcohol. That could be a blessing to people."

"Yeah, I know," he said. "I'm not ready yet."

"Okay," I told him. "Well, you'll do it when you're ready." I didn't want to push him. It wasn't my story; it was his.

We went downstairs and began speaking and singing a couple of songs. Then, all of a sudden, Billy started talking about his alcoholism. I turned around and looked at him in astonishment. Then I tried not to look too shocked because I didn't want the people to wonder why I was looking at him like that! But all the while I was thinking, "Gosh. Well, okay. Praise the Lord."

Billy went on and shared his story, and when the program was over Billy had about ten people lined up to talk to him. One man came over to him in tears and said, "Oh, my God! You came here for me today. You came here to talk to me."

When Billy shares about his struggle with alcohol, the number of people who flock to him when we're finished is amazing. It's both sexes, all races, and all ages.

---

* Up, Up, and Away: How We Found Love, Faith, and Lasting Marriage in the Entertainment World *by Marilyn McCoo, Billy Davis, Jr., and Mike Yorkey. Chicago: Moody Publishers, 2004. Used by permission of Moody Publishers.*

Prayer gave me the strength to get through that time in our lives, to stick with Billy through all of his struggles. We came very close to really ending our marriage. It was even after we had both come to the Lord. One time, he did something that really upset me. I said to him, "I'm really concerned about what you're doing. You don't act like you care about yourself, and now you're acting like you don't care about me. I don't know how much longer I'll be able to take this."

That was as much of an ultimatum as I could give him. I was speaking in truth when I said "I don't know how much longer I'll be able to take this." Shortly after that he stopped drinking.

The Lord gave me the patience. I prayed about Billy and his drinking all the time after I came to the Lord. Before I was praying, I tried to handle it through arguing. Prayer worked much better than arguing. It helped me tremendously. I learned not to take matters into my own hands.

One of my favorite Scriptures is in Philippians 4. It's verses 6 and 7 that speak to me most powerfully:

> Be anxious for nothing; but in every thing by prayer
> and supplication with thanksgiving let your requests
> be made known unto God. And the peace of God,
> which passeth all understanding, shall keep your
> hearts and minds through Christ Jesus.
> [Philippians 4:6-7 KJV]

I have to remember that part about being anxious for nothing. Every time I find myself being really upset and anxious, I know that I'm not turning it over to the Lord. Verse 6 also says that in all things, by prayer and supplication with thanksgiving, let your requests be made known to God. I wasn't letting my requests be known, either. Once I did that, then His peace took over.

I think Billy was praying a lot about his drinking, too. But some of those things are very personal. Billy still is a private individual. He'll share some things with me, but some things I have to leave between him and God.

I have to honor that. I don't have to know everything.

I try to start my day in prayer every morning, first thing before the phone starts ringing and before the distractions come along. If I get up before Billy, I usually go into my bathroom, get on my knees on the floor and pray with my elbows on the tub or on my side when my knees start hurting. If I wake up at night and can't sleep, I pray in bed. If I didn't have a chance to pray in the morning, I get in the car and pray.

I try to be flexible enough to make prayer fit into my life. You can pray with your hands in the sink washing dishes. You can pray anywhere. It's about where your focus is. The Bible tells us to pray without ceasing, and I try to do that.

Two or three mornings a week, Billy and I pray together. I like that a lot. We pray out loud. We just kneel with our elbows on the edge of the bed. Usually we'll start out just honoring the Lord.

We usually pray anywhere from twenty minutes to a half hour. We take turns speaking. One of us will start and then the other one will think of something and jump in. It helps to keep our focus on things and really function more as one. I get a chance to find out anything that might be of concern on his heart.

When I pray by myself I start off with the same pattern,

but I don't know where my prayer's going to go. Some-times I'm just really troubled that I don't feel like my focus is strong enough on the Lord. I wouldn't necessarily pray about things like that with Billy because I don't want to sad-dle him with my own personal problems that I feel like I'm having with the Lord.

Some things you just need to work out with the Lord by yourself. There are certain things you want to do with your man; there are certain things you want to do with God; and there are certain things that God expects you to take care of yourself.

I have prayed to God about being angry. I said, "Oh Lord, I'm so mad. Father, I know I'm not supposed to be mad, but I don't know how to handle this. Lord, if there's another way for me to look at this situation, would You show it to me so that I can change my feelings?"

I cannot tell you how many times He's answered that prayer! One day, I had a girlfriend who I'd been trying to get together with for lunch, for almost two years. Every time it would look like we would get something together, she'd cancel. On this particular day, she had just canceled again. I was driving and I said, "Lord, I am so pissed off. I know I'm supposed to be trying to get together with her, but Lord, I'm not motivated anymore. I just feel like she doesn't want to get together. She's hurting my feelings and I don't want to be bothered with it. Now, if there's another way I should be looking at this, please show me."

I just pray to God like I'm speaking honestly and realis-tically with Him. I'm not trying to be flowery. He already knows how I feel, so I put it out there.

On this particular day, within five minutes, all of a sudden the thought comes to me—maybe she's having a problem with her husband. Maybe this or that is going on. Within a very short period of time, He showed me three other possibilities that could be happening in her life that I had not considered. All I was thinking about was how she was making me feel.

That's the way He communicates with me. He'll place thoughts in my mind that I know are not my thoughts. As He showed them to me, my attitude changed completely, "Oh, I'm so sorry, Father. Oh, I never even realized that. Oh, that poor woman. Oh, I'll have to call her again."

In the beginning my prayers tended to be more selfish, more focused on what I needed and the people I cared about. I was not focusing on what God wants, what God is looking for from me.

That changed when Billy started a praise ministry about eight years ago called Soldiers for the Second Coming. Twice a month we get together. We have a musical group and sing praise songs. People come, sing songs with us, and some people get up and give testimonies or explain what the Lord has done in their lives.

What has changed about my prayers is spending less time asking for things for me and my loved ones. Today, I spend more time just praising God. A friend of ours said it so beautifully, "The only thing that we have to give God is praise because He owns everything else. Everything else is His."

Baptism

"Would you like to get engaged?" Grant asked me casually, as if it were nothing. We were studying together on a December afternoon in a small economics department office made available for graduate students at Oxford. The thought of being separated for the six-week long Christmas holiday break felt like forever. We had been inseparable for six months. He wanted to solidify our relationship, but he was smart not to use the word "marriage" or make it a big deal. He must have sensed that he would have scared me off.

I hid behind his chair and sent up an answer like a smoke signal. "Yes, I'd like that," I said from a crouching position. So we were engaged.

We'd met playing squash through friends. I thought we played at about the same level, but later found out he'd been sandbagging. He was one of the best players at Trinity College, where we both were students. After our second squash game he asked me out to breakfast.

"Where shall we go?" I asked.

"We could go to the pub for eggs, bacon, and fry-bread. Or," he said with a gleam in his eye, "we could have ice cream for breakfast." I was enchanted by his New Zealand accent and his invitation to do something sweetly wicked.

We bought our ice cream and sat on the grass in a small park to eat. It was late in spring and flowers were in bloom everywhere. We talked about the gardens and he actually knew the names of flowers: Primulas, Nasturtiums, Pansies and more. I was impressed by his strength, brains, and tenderness.

His kindness penetrated my numbness. One evening, as we ate dinner together, he asked me questions about my past. I matter-of-factly answered him with descriptions of having my leg amputated, my abusive stepfather, and the death of my real father who I never knew. He pushed back his plate and tears ran down his face. I was touched. I had no compassion for myself, but his tender affection impressed me. I did not know that I was still too emotionally stunted to reciprocate. I wasn't capable of having a relationship with a man without getting stuck in patterns from the past.

After becoming officially engaged and selecting rings, we went back home to our parents in separate countries for Christmas.

"This is the last time we will ever have to be apart for Christmas," he told me.

After Christmas, on his way from New Zealand back to England, Grant was able to stop in California and meet my family in San Diego. His decency, intelligence, and charm won over my mother quickly. Since Grant's parents were already planning to travel to England in June for his graduation with a D.Phil. in mathematics, we decided to hold the wedding in San Diego so they could participate on their way back to New Zealand.

Grant's parents wouldn't be able to afford another trip out of New Zealand for many years. Whereas I had the Rhodes Scholarship paying my Oxford tuition, Grant's parents had lived frugally for years, paying his tuition from their dairy farm. I admired Grant's ability to make it on a tight budget and persevere to reach his goal of an Oxford doctorate.

While Grant was in San Diego, he and I went to talk with Father Edelman, the chaplain I knew from Bishop's School. He now presided over a beautiful church made with old, gray stonework and pre-Raphaelite stained glass windows on Coronado Island. Whereas so much in California was new and modern, this felt traditional and connected to a rich past.

"Have you been baptized?" Father Edelman asked Grant.

"I was dedicated as a baby," he answered, "but never baptized as an adult."

"Well, as long as one of you has been baptized, we can still move forward," Father Edelman said.

Once we left his office I said to Grant, "Whew! That was close. My brother and sister were baptized while I was in the hospital. I missed it. He just assumed that I was baptized because I was in altar guild with him. Good thing it's not going to be a problem."

"Why don't we just get baptized?" Grant suggested. I was willing to pull the wool over the pastor's eyes, but Grant wanted to do the right thing. So we did.

Once we were back at Oxford we met with the Trinity College chaplain, Reverend Trevor ("Rev Trev"), and arranged for a series of eight weekly classes leading to baptism.

We had an intellectual, historical, and cultural discussion about the Bible and God. He didn't ask me uncomfortable questions, like whether I actually prayed. We kept everything on a mental, not emotional, level.

We completed the classes, got our Anglican baptismal certificates, and were able to walk down the aisle with a clean conscience. In this, as in so many areas of our relationship, Grant took the lead to help me become a better person, not just a person who achieved things. I looked up to Grant and wanted to make him happy.

My mother gave us a big, beautiful, white wedding. The reception was hosted by a friend of hers at the officer's club on Coronado Island, right on the edge of the beach. We packed the church with African Americans, New Zealanders, a crowd of Jewish relatives, and English friends from Oxford.

Kelly Hoke

Kelly Hoke waited at her husband Wynn's office for him to finish work. She overheard someone say to him, "Have you talked to her yet?"

"Ummm. No, not yet," her husband answered. "I will."

Kelly looked from one to the other. "What is going on?" she asked her husband.

"Um, well, honey . . . it looks like I am going to Iraq in May," he told her hesitantly.

"What?" Kelly shook her head, hoping she had heard wrong. "No, you're kidding right? This is a joke."

"No, I am really not kidding," her husband said. "And, yes, I am going."

"But you just got home February 6. You were gone 545 days in Afghanistan. How can they send you out again in May?"

Wynn tried to explain. "They really need me. They don't have enough people who do my line of work." Wynn is a counselor in the military.

"That is just nuts," said Kelly. "I have to go outside. I need a few minutes alone." She didn't want to lose control in his office in front of everyone.

Kelly sat in her car and started to cry. She didn't expect to hear that he was shipping out again after only ninety days at home. She didn't expect to find out in a public place, either. One of the lieutenants came out and passed nearby. He saw her in the car and asked, "Are you okay?"

"I'm okay," Kelly answered with tears in her eyes.

"Is your husband going to Iraq?" he asked.

"Yes," she said. "I just found out five minutes ago."

"Oh, I am so sorry," he told her. "I gotta tell you: Our soldiers, they go over there and they serve our country and they do a good job. But I think the most patriotic people are the people who are left here, the families."

I never thought of myself as serving our country. My husband serves our country, but I never thought of myself as serving, too.

While Wynn is away, prayer is a great help. It helps to talk to God about my daily issues. It helps knowing that He has a plan and that I am going through all of these things because He knows I am capable. With prayer, I didn't have that sense of despair that my husband was going to go over there and not come home. I just knew that God did not bring us together to take him away from me.

I was so tired of kissing toads before I met Wynn. I told God, "I'm done dating. I want to take a sabbatical and hang out with my family and my friends. I know that You have a good man out there, a man of God who believes the same things that I do so we can have a good marriage together." I just turned it over to God. And then I met Wynn.

I am really, really fortunate. He's an awesome family

man. He's a hard worker and he's dedicated to his country. I'm so proud of him.

I don't watch the news on TV about what's happening in Iraq. I just stay in touch with Wynn by phone. I am so lucky to hear his voice and know that he is healthy and fine. One time, though, I remember hearing all of these sirens in the background while we were talking on the phone. Wynn said, "I gotta go! I gotta go!"

I asked him what was going on and he just yelled, "I gotta go! I gotta hit the bunkers! They're lobbing in missiles!" and he hung up the phone.

I was left holding the phone at work . . . stunned. I fell apart. I thought I was going to lose my mind. I got permission to take the rest of the day off. I went and rode my horse and cleared my head. That's when I feel close to God and I pray. I love to be outdoors, in nature and with our animals. That's where I go when I need some strength. It heals me.

Nature reminds me of why we're here; it reminds me of God. Here in Texas, we have white-tailed deer that come in our backyard. I see two or three, sometimes even sixteen deer grazing. I put out birdseed for a male and female cardinal. There are two skunks that stop by. Nature is my sanctuary. I get so inspired. I have my hands full with Wynn over there. We have horses, dogs, and birds to care for.

I pray two ways. With Wynn over there, I catch myself praying "Help me, help me," all the time instead of being thankful. But when I am out in nature that helps me focus on being thankful to God. It's what keeps me grounded.

I used to pray with an expectation, telling God "this is what I need" or asking for help with specific things. I realize that I was always telling God what to do, giving God a "to do" list. Now I deal with uncertainty more easily. It works much better when I open my heart and let God teach me how to live.

I'm *really* not looking forward to Wynn going to Iraq. I was talking to one of his superiors and he was telling me that where he is going is not as intense as some of the other places he could go. That gives me some reassurance. But I just have to continue to tell myself—I cry when I think about it—that God brought us together for a reason and I know he'll come home. He came home once, and I know he'll come home again.

The West Wing

"The National Economic Council left a message for you on the answering machine," Grant told me. "I think they want you to give a speech." Grant and I had moved from Oxford to San Diego. He worked at Scripps Institute of Oceanography and I worked in sales for IBM. I had decided against working on Wall Street in favor of a business career that I thought would be more flexible for starting a family. Instead of looking for security by making a lot of money in stocks and bonds, I looked toward building a family as my sense of security and stability.

I dialed the number from the message. It rang and rang and rang. Finally, someone answered.

"Hi, I'm returning a call from the NEC," I said. "I think they want me to give a speech?"

"Well, this is the switchboard for the West Wing of the White House. For the NEC you need to talk to Sylvia Mathews. Let me try her line." I sat in stunned silence, surprised to find that I was calling the White House!

Sylvia Mathews had been a student at Oxford while I was

there. She had worked on President Clinton's campaign. In October, after the election, she asked a friend of hers to collect resumes of people who might come to work in the Clinton Administration. I was approached to submit a resume, along with many other people we knew. Now in February—four months later—I had completely forgotten about sending it in.

"Sylvia Mathews," she answered at last. "May I help you?"

"Hello, it's Bonnie St. John, returning your call."

"Great! Are you interested in coming here to work for the NEC? We'd like to interview you."

Sylvia and I talked more about the NEC, a new department in the White House formed by the Clinton team to raise economic issues, both global and domestic, to the level of the National Security Council. I told Sylvia I was interested in interviewing for the job. She said she would set it up and call me back in a few days.

I was excited about the possibility of a job in the White House, but I worried about my marriage. Grant and I agreed that I should go through the interviews and do my best. We could begin to think about our options. We didn't have to make a decision unless they actually offered the job to me.

The next time I managed to reach Sylvia she told me she had set up several interviews for Thursday—and it was already Tuesday. When I looked for flights to D.C. all I could find was a ticket that cost about two-thirds of my monthly take-home pay at IBM. The government would not be reimbursing me for the trip. I decided to go ahead and take a leap of faith.

I presented myself at one of the small white security booths built into the black iron fence surrounding the White House. After checking my ID and running my Social Security number, they issued me a temporary ID which hung on a chain around my neck, and allowed me to walk down the wide driveway next to the main front lawn, bypassing the grand columns on the front of the White House in favor of the smaller porch of the West Wing entrance.

Marines stood at attention, not blinking, smiling, or turning to look at me as I moved toward the door. Inside, the small lobby was decorated in conservative taste: oriental rugs, a glass cabinet of vases, antique furniture, and an ornate reception desk.

After a few minutes, Sylvia came out to talk. Unfortunately, she told me, I had lost my time slots with the three senior officials I needed to meet because the funeral for Thurgood Marshall, the civil rights activist and Supreme Court Justice, was being held today. Everyone's schedule was being rearranged.

"You'll have to wait here until they have a free moment and can see you. I'm sorry, but this could take a while. It's the best I can do," she said apologetically.

I settled in to wait. From where I sat, I could watch everyone come and go. Hillary Clinton went by. Al Gore breezed through. Lots of prominent people were here for the funeral. Thinking of all the presidents, world leaders, and great thinkers who had passed through these doors, I felt awe.

Over the course of about six hours, Sylvia managed to squeeze me in to meetings with Bob Rubin the National Economic Adviser (who later became Secretary of the Treasury), and his deputy assistants Bo Cutter and Gene Sperling. They were tough on me.

"Why didn't you graduate with a summa cum laude degree from Harvard?" asked Bob. "You only got magna cum laude. You could have tried harder."

"Only a silver medal in skiing?" asked Gene. "Why not the gold?"

It was good preparation for a world where reporters would line up to criticize the president, his staff, and his policies. Once you entered the White House, nothing you did went without criticism, no matter how great the achievement.

In the third interview, Bo Cutter explained his vision of the NEC.

"In today's economy we have new problems," said Bo passionately. "Our workforce has to compete with workers around the world. Money flows across borders in the blink of an eye." He leaned back. "Yet our government departments haven't changed since World War II. The NEC must be a nimble group that can quickly pull together people from across the government to solve today's new economic problems." I was inspired by Bo's vision of the NEC. All the economics I had studied at Harvard and Oxford came to life. I felt I could make a difference.

It was a few days after I went home that I found out—yes! They were really asking me to come to work for President Clinton in the White House! My joy was only dampened by the feeling that I had to choose between my marriage and a job in the White House.

My first instinct was to analyze the problem logically. Asking Grant to move to D.C. didn't make a lot of sense. He was on track to earn tenure at Scripps, one of the best oceanographic research institutes in the world. Without knowing whether I would like national politics or whether national politics would like me, giving up his opportunity at Scripps wasn't fair.

Yet, going away to D.C. without him for a year or two was unthinkable to me. I was prepared to say, "No thanks." I would not do anything that could jeopardize our marriage, which formed my grounding and purpose in life. I still had no relationship with God. My world revolved around marriage and loyalty to my husband. If he had told me not to go, I would not have gone.

But Grant urged me to go to Washington. "I don't want to have a bitter wife one day when she realizes she passed up the opportunity of a lifetime," he said. He argued that we could commute by plane, talk on the phone, and keep our marriage going long distance.

Military couples had to do it all the time, he pointed out. They didn't have the luxury of daily phone calls lasting for hours like we would. Grant suggested that we agree to a commuter marriage for two years—a reasonable period to hold a job—and then decide which person should relocate. We agreed that once we were living on the same coast again, we would start a family.

I was afraid of being so far away from my husband for so long. Emotionally, I was very dependent on Grant. A psychologist explained to me that being abused as a child ruptures one's fundamental sense of security. In the absence of healing the damage, a person will either feel threatened all the time and be unable to function as an adult or learn to compensate by creating a workable situation that makes you feel secure while covering up the emotional abyss below.

Being married was my way of gaining security and avoiding my own emotions. In exchange for that, I was willing to let Grant decide things like whether or not I went to work in the White House. We appeared to be two independent, intelligent adults in a relationship; but in reality, I was emotionally dependent in an unhealthy way.

Christine Todd Whitman

Christine Todd Whitman, former head of the Environmental Protection Agency (EPA) under President George W. Bush and former governor of New Jersey, has had to face up to media firestorms and political battles throughout her career.

Probably the most well known battle is over the EPA's statement regarding the air quality in lower Manhattan following the 9/11 terrorist attacks. Seven days following the attacks, on September 18, 2001, the EPA released a statement that said: "We are very encouraged that the results from our monitoring of air quality and drinking water conditions in both New York and near the Pentagon show that the public in these areas is not being exposed to excessive levels of asbestos or other harmful substances," Christine said. "And given the scope of the tragedy from last week, I am glad to reassure the people of New York and Washington, D.C., that their air is safe to breathe and their water is safe to drink," she added.*

However, despite the fact that the air and water were safe

Environmental Protection Agency, Press Release, www.EPA.gov. September 18, 2001.

for the public, Whitman and other officials repeatedly warned recovery workers on the sites to wear respirators, recognizing that the air on these sites was still dangerous.

With regard to New York in particular, the statement was directed to the residents in and around lower Manhattan, but it has been erroneously interpreted by some to have covered even the responders working directly on Ground Zero.

Thus, the EPA was accused of downplaying the potential health hazards for rescue workers after 9/11. Some accused the Bush Administration of editing the scientific findings in press releases from the EPA, and directing the EPA to tone down warnings. More than five years later, Christine is still in the hot seat.

In a *60 Minutes** interview with Katie Couric, Christine said, "We did everything we could to protect people from that environment and we did it in the best way that we could, which was to communicate with those people who had the responsibility for enforcing (the use of respirators)," Whitman said. "We didn't have the authority to do that enforcement, but we communicated (the need to wear respirators) to the people who did," she said. "(In) no uncertain terms (city officials were warned of the danger). EPA was very firm in what it communicated and it did communicate up and down the line."

Many of the estimated 40,000 workers—firefighters, police, construction and other workers—who recovered bodies and cleaned the World Trade Center ruins have health problems. Anger and criticism—even charges of lying—have been aimed at Christine and the EPA for not emphasizing the danger enough and for declaring New York's air quality as safe.

When Couric said that many of the first responders heard the

*CBS. 60 Minutes *Interview of Gov. Christine Todd Whitman with Katie Couric on September 10, 2006. Transcript from CBS.com.*

air was safe and that this gave them a false sense of security, Christine responded "You know, it's hard to know when people hear what they want to hear. And there's so much going on that maybe they didn't make the distinction." Whitman never said the air was safe on the pile at Ground Zero.

Christine told Couric, "The last thing in the world that I would ever do would be to put people at risk," she said. "You want to say, 'You're wrong. I mean, you're just so wrong.' We never lied."

"The readings (in lower Manhattan) were showing us that there was nothing that gave us any concern about long-term health implications," she told Couric. "That was different from on the pile itself, at Ground Zero. There, we always said consistently, 'You've got to wear protective gear.'"

Christine believes her faith has been a vital factor in her ability to deal with negative publicity and criticism. Prayer has supported her in making this and other difficult decisions over the course of her career, as well as living with the impact of those decisions.

My son was in building seven at the World Trade Center on 9/11. He got out. He will be affected forever, obviously, but he got out, and that's the most important thing. But I had to be able to provide some strength for the people who had relatives, families, loved ones, who didn't get out.

Then, on top of that, people who worked for the Port Authority of New York and New Jersey, that I had put in that position, were in harm's way. I lost several good friends that day.

That was a time, certainly, when I prayed for the strength to know what to do—how to reach out to the widows, how to have the strength to be a support for them, and not stop and think about my own pain. In comparison, what I faced was minimal.

And we all had to go on, because we had an important job to do with the EPA. We had to go on and do that with honesty and clarity and forthrightness that balanced everybody's needs and the realities of the world.

When making any decision, my guide is to do what I think is right. If I do that, I just don't listen to all the criticism that goes on all around. I hear it—and never really develop what they call a "thick skin" or get to the point that it doesn't bother me. Of course, it does.

What really bothers me most is when people go after my motives for a decision.

Prayer helps me deal with that; at the end of the day, it's what gets me through. Even when you're clear in your conscience—and really, conscience to me is that inner feeling with God—you have to understand that other people will still challenge your decisions and attribute bad motives to you. I just have to say, "Okay, let's forgive them and get on with it. I'm comfortable and I know where I am."

I am still being sued about the EPA statement. It doesn't go away. You just have to go on.

We live on a beautiful farm in New Jersey. There is a path through the woods that's a little over a mile. It takes us down through the woods and along the river . . . you see the sunlight shining through . . . you hear the birds and see many of the wild animals. You see God's hand in it all. I just take a deep breath and feel that it's an extraordinary world in which we live and we're very lucky to be here.

Every day that I get that opportunity to be in nature, I always thank God for the ability to enjoy all that I am given. I usually walk our dogs by myself. It's my private time, a very special time that's important to me. I give thanks for the family that I have and the strength of my family. I pray for the health and the strength of the people I know and the people around the world who are in desperate need of it. For me, it's mainly a thank you.

Nature can be a real antidote for some of the craziness of politics. It's the real world, as far as I'm concerned. You step back and you take a little time to absorb what's around you—not even think about it so much; but just absorb it.

I pray a little bit every day. I haven't ever done it by setting aside a certain time or having a prescribed way of doing it. At the end of the day, I try to get a little quiet peace, either when I'm in bed or when I get a chance to walk our three dogs.

I also pray at night. I have a ritual at night. It's taking time when I'm in bed to put everything else out of my mind, and give thanks. There are short prayers that I always say, that I learned as a child, and keep saying.

I believe in God above.
I believe in Jesus' love.
I believe that I should be kind and loving, Lord, like
    Thee.

That's the minimum that I will say every night. Then, depending on the day or the concerns or what's on my mind, I will say perhaps a more formal prayer, like The Lord's Prayer or the Nicene Creed. I also ask for God's blessings on people who I know and pray for people who I don't know. It's what I learned from my mother.

I don't think of it as prayer in the morning, but I always stop and think: "Thank You, it's another day." I think about what the teachings of the Bible are relative to my responsibility toward others. How do you manifest that in the course of a day? You look for opportunities. I think about that. It's not a formal prayer *per se*.

I do recite this in the woods from time to time. It was a saying that my grandmother had outside in a special place in her garden. She believed in prayer a lot and did a lot of it!

> The kiss of the sun for pardon,
> The songs of the birds for mirth,
> One is nearer God's heart in the garden
> Than anywhere else on earth!
> [Dorothy Frances Gurney]

It's just an old saying, but to me it's very true.

You don't necessarily need the formal structure of a building and you don't need an intermediary between you and God. But I do like to go to church. I like the ritual. Also, it gives you an hour every Sunday where God is exactly what you think about for one hour. I enjoy that, but I don't feel that it is necessary for my relationship to God.

In my jobs I have faced attacks and criticism. People sometimes judge my motives and presume I am a corrupt person. Prayer is one aspect that helps me stand in the middle of all that and stay sane. My interpretation of what would be expected of me in the teachings of the Bible is also very important in how I carry out what I do.

At the same time, though, I'm not looking in the Bible every day to find out what it would tell me to do here. It's just part of my makeup, my upbringing, in the sense that the teachings of Jesus are what tell you how to treat your fellow human beings. Those teachings very much form a basis for my actions and my decisions.

When it gets to be really rough with things that are of high importance, when a lot of people are second guessing you, you just have to get back to that place where you're in good conscience. For me, conscience means you are carrying out, you are living to the extent possible (understanding you can never be fully perfect) the biblical teachings with which you have been brought up.

If I had to choose one Bible verse that relates to how I feel about prayer, it would be the Twenty-third Psalm. It has the most meaning to me. I am a very strong *King James Version* person, so I love the poetry of it. It talks about how you can let God guide you and sustain you in difficult times: The LORD is my shepherd.

Making a Name for Myself

Bo Cutter called me into his office one morning a couple of weeks after I began my job as director for Human Capital on the National Economic Council.

"The Secretary of Labor called me," he said. "He wanted to know who Bonnie St. John is."

"Wow," I thought. "I've only been here a few weeks and the Secretary of Labor is recognizing my work."

"Secretary Reich was concerned about a memo you sent over to someone on his staff," Bo explained. "He feels the White House is becoming too involved with the Labor Department's business."

My face went red hot. Secretary Reich knew my name, but not in a good way. Not only had I ticked off a cabinet member, but one of the president's best friends. Legend had it that when they sailed over to England together on the QEII as Rhodes Scholars, Clinton became seasick and Reich nursed him.

Bo told me not to worry too much about it, but of course I did. I went home that night feeling disappointed with myself. I actually thought I could make a difference, but I couldn't even write a memo without getting slapped down.

This difficult political situation was nothing compared to the difficulties people like Christine Todd Whitman, Libby Pataki and Barbara Bush have faced in politics. When I interviewed them for this book I had so much empathy for the pressures they have withstood. Whether or not you agree with their decisions, I have to admire their courage as women to stand up in the limelight and take the heat. If, like them, I had relied on a foundation of prayer, I am sure I could have faced politics in a more grounded way.

Instead, my only emotional outlet was going to the gym and getting on the StairMaster. I pumped out my frustration. I told myself I was an idiot for coming to work in Washington. Without support from Reich, I wouldn't be able to get anything done. I thought about going home. I stayed on that StairMaster for over an hour, continuing to sweat out my annoyance at myself. I slept well.

The next morning, I went back to work. I held my head high and began again. I set out to build relationships of trust at various levels in the Labor Department. I found ways to help them with their initiatives, from welfare reform to NAFTA. By the time I actually left the White House, Secretary Reich invited me to lunch in his private office to say good-bye. He knew my name, and it was a good thing. We had made friends.

The biggest personal thing that happened during my time in Washington was when my mother's husband, Sidney, suddenly died of a heart attack. Susan Rice, a friend of mine from Oxford who worked at the NEC one floor up from me, was very sympathetic. She knew my family and had met Sidney before. She immediately cleared her schedule and offered to be with me for the evening before I went back to California for the funeral.

She came over to my apartment to console me. Sidney had been married to my mom for fifteen years. He cheered for me at the Olympics, came to my graduation from Harvard, and gave me away when I married Grant. He was the best dad I ever had.

After trying to console me for a while, Susan looked at me funny and said, "You aren't really feeling anything, are you?"

"No," I admitted. "Not really." I felt awful for not feeling more, like at my father's funeral. All my life I had acted according to the emotions people expected from me. This was, however, the first time that I remember someone actually telling me the truth about myself.

"That's very strange," Susan said.

When Susan, who knew me well, looked at me and told me my reactions weren't normal, it was my first inkling of how emotionally cut off I was. Still, I didn't make the connection that childhood abuse had stifled my emotional life.

I went to Sidney's funeral and then returned to D.C. I worked at the White House for almost a year and a half before returning to San Diego with the intention of having a baby and making a family with Grant. I did not know the obstacles I faced at home and inside myself were greater than the obstacles in the outside world.

Barbara Bush

It is former first lady Barbara Bush, mother of president of the United States, George W. Bush, and former governor of Florida, Jeb Bush, that was reportedly responsible for teaching the Bush children their life lessons. While the future president was building a name for himself in the oil business, and eventually on the national political stage, Mrs. Bush was a passionately attentive mother who raised her kids according to a set of rules that one relative calls "Barbara's principles." "The Bush children were expected to look beyond themselves and be mindful of the needs of the less fortunate. To keep their whining to themselves, and to never take themselves too seriously."[*]

Ganny, as she is known to her seventeen grandchildren, is said to enforce the same standards today. The "grands" have reportedly nicknamed their annual summer trip to the Bush family's Kennebunkport, Maine, home "boot camp" because of Barbara's strict rules.

---

[*] *"The Queen Mother" by Martha Brant and Weston Kosova in* Newsweek, *May 13, 2002, U.S. Edition, pg. 34. Copyright 2002.*

There are reportedly "Pick up your towels," and "Don't leave your clothes on the floor," warning notices tacked to the bedroom doors.

Unlike the first ladies who came before and after her, Barbara has cultivated a maternal public persona and has gladly left politics to her then-president husband and her now-president son. She is the first woman since Abigail Adams, wife of second US president John Adams, to have been wife to one president and mother to another.* Barbara would like to be remembered for her work in the fight against illiteracy, caring for others, and above all else, the love she has for her family.

She is close to the current president, George W., and is said to call him often to offer encouragement or a funny joke when she feels he needs a lift. Mother and son have always used humor to deal with life's inevitable difficulties. George and Barbara went through a very painful time following the death of their second child, three-year-old daughter Robin, born Pauline Robinson Bush, to leukemia in 1953. George W., then just a child himself, reportedly stayed close to his mother's side and often tried to cheer her up with jokes. Barbara says that during that period she and her husband really learned what "Thy will be done" meant. Prayer, especially those of family and friends, played an important role in helping her through that experience.

I'm not good at talking about religion or prayer. But I do believe in the power of prayer.

I have a friend who told me she prays for my son George every day. I said to her, "Well, please continue, because he feels your prayers. He tells me he feels your prayers."

My friend said, "I know that's true. I had a mastectomy

* *"The Queen Mother" by Martha Brant and Weston Kosova in* Newsweek, *May 13, 2002, U.S. Edition, pg. 34. Copyright 2002.*

operation and all my friends got a prayer group going. They prayed for me. When it was over and I was well, when they stopped praying . . . I felt that they had stopped praying."

I believe that. The power of those prayers was so strong that she felt it, and when the cancer left, she felt them stop praying. I believe you can feel it when people are praying for you.

About two years ago, I read a book called *A Sundog Moment*,* by Sharon Baldacci, who was diagnosed with multiple sclerosis twenty-one years ago. She is the sister of the very talented mystery writer, David Baldacci. It's a novel about a woman who has MS and has a terrible time coping with it. Her family fussed over her. They were so solicitous; she didn't like that. So many things were difficult. She finally discovered that if she thanked God all during the day for the things that are good in her life it made everything else easier. That changed her life. That changed my life.

Again, prayer is something very hard for me to talk about. Episcopalians are the "frozen chosen" they say. But when I'm sitting on the ocean looking at a sparkling beautiful day, surrounded by family and friends, I take time, now, to thank God for those things. That's what I want to say about how I pray. That's what I have learned.

I think I'm the luckiest woman in the world because I married the most wonderful man, I have five great children, and I've got seventeen wonderful grandchildren. And I love my in-laws, too. So I'm pretty lucky. It's not to say we're all perfect. We all have problems, but they'e solvable. I am blessed.

I feel the negatives when others criticize the people I love. But I'm grown up enough to know that many of the things they say about the people I love are not true. I'm not quite so grown

---

* A Sundog Moment: A Novel of Hope *by Sharon Baldacci. New York: Center Street, 2004.*

up, though, to always see that the things they say are not true about the people who I don't love. I have to learn to do that.

When I am asked what advice I would give my grand-children about prayer, I find that giving my grandchildren advice is not as good as setting an example. Kids don't do what we tell them; they do what we do.

I would like them to see that we never avoid prayer. We say our prayers and we are grateful for what we have. Prayer and church are big things in our lives. I was brought up going to church on Sundays and we still go. We say blessings before meals. My husband and I say our prayers every night.

I want them to see us living a good life, which is what their grandfather and I *try* to do: decency, honesty, being kind to others, and sharing. I think it's made a difference in the lives of our children. You can talk about all those things, but unless they see you doing it, it just doesn't make too much of an impression.

For our own lives, prayer has made a huge difference. When you get to be eighty-one and eighty-two, if you have faith, fear of death goes away.

One of my favorite parts of the Bible is the Beatitudes. I love,

> Blessed are the poor in spirit:
> for theirs is the kingdom of heaven.
> Blessed are the meek:
> for they shall possess the land.
> (Matthew 5: 1-2 NIV)

I love those. I love the Beatitudes, and I'm trying to live my life by them.

Endings and Beginnings

"Hello!" said Amy, when we bumped into each other in the food court at the local mall. "How are you?" she asked. I used to work with her at IBM San Diego. We hadn't seen each other in a long time.

"We're great." I laughed pointing at my large belly. It was easy to see that I was already six months pregnant.

"So your job in the White House ended?" she asked. Last time she'd seen me, I was leaving IBM to start work at the National Economic Council.

"Yes, I left in April and moved back to San Diego."

"Where are you working now?" Amy asked.

"Actually, I'm writing a book," I told her. I was glad that I was wearing my businesslike black and white houndstooth maternity suit. It looked more professional than a muumuu-style maternity dress. I wanted to be taken seriously.

"A book?" I saw doubt begin to creep into her eyes. "What's it about?"

"It's motivational. It's called, *Succeeding Sane*."

"Uh-huh. I see." It was clear she did not see. "Who's your publisher?"

"I don't have a publisher yet. I'm still working on the proposal."

"I see," she said. She saw 165 pounds of houndstooth with no job pretending to be an author. She smiled indulgently at me, the way you would to a small child or a mentally challenged adult. "That's so nice!"

I had seen that look in people's eyes many times in the five months since I left the White House. Before, I had automatic respect as a White House economic official with a gold-embossed business card. Now I was a big blimp.

"I wish my self-esteem wasn't so tied up in work," I thought to myself. I didn't want to continue working ninety hours per week, like I did at the White House, and never see my child. I wanted to feel proud of making the commitment to being a mother and being at home. Instead, I felt insecure and apologetic about my choices.

Without any connection to God, I needed achievements, a fancy job title, or a big salary to feel good about myself. I didn't have a sense of my own value as a child of God.

PART IV

MOTHERHOOD AND WORKING WITH THE SPIRIT

Janet Parshall

It was 3:00 a.m. when Janet Parshall, nationally syndicated radio talk show host, and her husband, Craig, were awakened from a deep sleep by a knock on the door. Disoriented and bleary eyed, she stumbled to the bedroom window where she could see two men in uniform standing in her driveway. She shook her husband awake, "Craig, I think there are two policemen down there!"

Heading down the stairs, they opened the door to find two ashen-faced state troopers staring back at them. "Do you have a son named Sam?"

"Yes," they answered in unison, breathless, their hearts pounding.

"He's been shot in the head. We don't know if he's dead or alive."

Janet immediately began to pray: "Father, I praise You that Sam knows You as Lord and Savior. If he is gone, I rejoice that he's in Your presence. If he's not, we're three hours away from the hospital and I thank You, because You, the great physician, are already there and have been on duty all night long. Let me now be a witness to these officers who might not yet know You as Lord and Savior."

Sam was away at college. He and his roommate had just ordered pizza and planned to watch a movie. His roommate had been given a gun by his father for protection. Sam had never seen a gun up close. There were no guns in the Parshall household and he was not especially impressed.

"Let's just eat and watch the movie," Sam said. But just as he turned to look at the television, *Bang!* The gun suddenly discharged.

The gun had been so close to Sam's head that there were flash burns on his ear. At first, the police officers thought that he had been shot execution-style because of the close-range of the gunshot. Considering the circumstances, Sam should be dead.

But the doctors were stupefied. The bullet went in, literally did a U-turn, and came out on the same side.

The next eighteen months were a non-stop prayer vigil for Sam. With a traumatic head injury it was impossible to know at what point the patient would plateau. They weren't sure whether Sam would ever be able to walk or talk or think or smell or taste again. He had aphasia like a stroke victim. Janet's motivation to pray was stronger than it had ever been.

Eventually, after the shooting, Sam went through rehab. He had to be taught to walk and talk again. Janet praises God that everything came back. He married, got his master's degree in film, and has given Janet and her husband two beautiful granddaughters thus far. And, except for a serpentine scar on the back of his head, you would never look at Sam and say, *"That boy's been shot."*

Sam is now twenty-eight years old. When he's visiting his parents and Janet gets a moment alone with him, she'll take him and squish him in front of a mirror, and say, "Now Sammy, what do you see?"

And he'll say, "A walking, talking miracle."

And she'll say, "And don't you ever forget it."

Janet says the experience taught her an important lesson. She was able to say "Lord, in my mortal's perception, parents should die before children, not the other way around. But You are on the throne; I'm not. I bow in submission. My children were always Yours, just like every other blessing in my life."

I truly believe it was the hand of God put in the path of that bullet and the Lord said, "Not now." That it was not Sam's appointed time to die.

God could've answered my prayer that night in a way that said "I'm taking him home." One of the things I realized in my experience with Sam's shooting is that that little boy never belonged to me. And that realization really shook some of my core beliefs. I have the stretch marks and I carried him for nine months, but here's the reality: the Lord gave me and his daddy permission to mold and shape his heart and his mind. Whether or not Sam would get three score and ten years was completely before the throne of grace; his mother and father were not the final arbiters of that decision.

Over my life that hasn't always been the easiest lesson to learn. Even though I am the host of my own national radio show, known for defending the family as a conservative Christian, my babies are my Achilles heel. If I'm gonna be attacked by the father of lies, it always comes through my children. I think Satan knows that's my biggest point of vulnerability. And I think prior to Sam's gunshot wound, there was this feeling that because I had carried my children there was a sense of ownership. Turning over my babies to God is the hardest thing for me to do.

I have been praying all my life. I pray first thing in the morning, with my husband, if I can. I also pray last thing at night. And I pray during my hour and a half commute both into D.C.

and back home. I'm really in constant communication with Him throughout the day. My mama said it beautifully, "There is no final Amen until we're standing in His presence."

Before my feet hit the bedroom floor in the morning I want to spend time talking with Him. Even if I'm walking through a valley or experiencing a difficult time, I try to start out first by praising Him and thanking Him. Usually, my opening line is: "This is the day which the Lord has made; let us rejoice and be glad in it" (Psalm 118:24 RSV).

The fact that I opened my eyes and drew a breath meant that the Lord said: "There is still something that I'd like you to join me in working for." I could've gone to glory in the night. The fact that I woke up and I'm still here is such a profound reminder that I didn't get up to go to work, I didn't get up to pay my bills, I didn't get up to do my laundry—I got up to honor and glorify Him and to commune with Him.

Beginning the day with prayer has had a profound effect on my life, even if I'm in the refiner's fire. I pray every morning, if only for ten minutes. It takes the focus off the fire and puts the focus on the Father instead. The Scripture says that my God shall supply all my needs, according to his riches and glory, through Christ Jesus (see Philippians 4:19). So prayer isn't about alerting Him to my needs, it's about my heart being changed.

Next, I pray for my family, wherever they are in life, whatever they're doing. It's very precious for me to end the prayer by turning over and looking at my husband, if he's not yet awake, and thanking God for him in particular. He's my high school sweetheart. We've been married thirty-five years, and I never, ever, take for granted that that face is still looking at me in the morning.

If Craig is awake we pray together. It's the most intimate thing a husband and wife can do. I have made that statement on the air of my radio show, and I've had it confirmed by great Bible teachers who have also written books on prayer. You can't have a grudge against your mate, be spewing insults, and then suddenly say, "And now we'll put on our Sunday school face and talk to God."

I adore my husband Craig. He is brilliant and has the gift of wisdom and the gift of words. I love to hold his hand and let him lead when we pray. He inevitably says exactly what's in my heart. I very rarely have to add a PS or a coda onto the prayer. And it lets me know exactly where he's at. We've been doing this for so many years as a married couple. It's just like talking to one another, only we're talking to our heavenly Father along with each other.

I also sometimes pray in the quietude of my car. It's wonderful; there's a whole big section of my commute where I'm going around the Blue Ridge Mountains, so I'm blocked on my cell phone. I can't be distracted even if I want to be. And in the car I can talk out loud to Him, as if He is my best friend and is sitting next to me.

I've gotten over the idea of ritualism with prayer. There's the ABC approach and the method that models the Lord's Prayer. I think it's important to go deeper than the formal prayers that we've been taught. Above all else, He listens to us and He wants to communicate with us.

If someone asked me what I've learned about prayer over the years, what I would want my grandchildren to know, the main thing I would say is that prayer needs to be simple. We think that prayers are more effective if they're highfalutin and verbose.

I would want my grandchildren to understand that there's a relational aspect to prayer. You are talking to your Abba, your heavenly Father who hears you. Even in baby talk, He still understands what you're saying. You can just say "Help." You can say, "Lord, I hurt too much to articulate the pain." If I can teach my grandbabies anything, I want them to step out of the ritualism and into a relationship.

If I could change anything in my own prayer life I would have spent more time saying "Thank You," rather than please. The Lord has never disappointed. I've never gone without food. He's blessed me with a marriage that's super glued together. I have these four precious children and an unbelievable opportunity through broadcasting. Yet, I think back on how many times I asked Him for something like He was the 24-hour convenience mart—as though all I had to do was ask Him and He would provide it. I look back and I think it would've been so much better on so many occasions if I had simply said "Thank You."

That's what I do at the end of the day, say prayers of thanksgiving. I thank Him for His grace in all of the things that happened during the day. Then I also ask Him for forgiveness for the times where I may have disappointed Him, where I may have been less than obedient, less than faithful. Because the work that I do is so public, if I besmirched the ambassadorship of my heirship I want to go back and ask Him to forgive me.

And Craig and I will pray together; it's a wonderful way to connect after we've gone our separate ways during the day. At the end of the day, prayer pulls us back to the same place.

My prayer today is often, Lord, give me faith enough to finish the race. It goes back to Hebrews 12:1–3, "Help me to run with perseverance." And the only way I can do that, without being exhausted, is by keeping my eyes on Jesus.

Mission—Hanukkah Party

BONNIE'S STORY

There was so much to do! I headed into Toys-R-Us with a list of the six kids who would be at the Hanukkah party for the Schwimmer family in San Diego. I had their genders, ages, and interests. Pushing my cart, I drove down each aisle with determination and purpose. The first two, the youngest, were the easiest: a doll and a stuffed animal. I asked for advice from the sales clerk about a gift for a four-year-old girl and we decided on a dress up kit with a boa, tiara, and toy high heels. In the boys department, I agonized over a chemistry set to make fake worms or walkie-talkies. Finally, after more than an hour, I raced to the other side of the store to find wrapping paper and bows in appropriate colors.

Well, perhaps "raced" is too strong a word. No one really "races" anywhere when they are eight and a half months pregnant. How fast can one waddle? I was eight and a half months pregnant . . . and with an artificial leg I was lucky to be walking at all.

It's a vicious circle. The more weight pregnant amputees gain, the worse their leg fits. The harder it is to walk, the less exercise they get and the more weight they gain.

I gained forty-two pounds. Since I'm only five feet two inches, that's a lot of weight. Darcy was only six pounds, nine ounces, so about thirty-five pounds was extra. I looked like a beach ball with head, hands, and an artificial leg rolling slowly through Toys-R-Us. But I was determined.

I did my limping waddle out to the car with my cart of gifts for Hanukkah. Ever since my mother married Sidney I had attended the big functions in our Jewish family. I felt it was really, really important that I go to the Hanukkah party. Or maybe I was just hormonal.

Grant was out of town for work, so there I was gingerly loading packages into the car one at a time. Then came an interesting challenge: getting into the car. Opening the door was easy. Sitting down was like doing a deep-knee bend on one leg at almost one hundred and seventy pounds. I braced my hands on the door and roof to slowly lower myself in.

Successfully wedged into the driver's seat, my next challenge was reaching the gas and brake pedals. I pulled the seat forward so that my stomach pushed up against the steering wheel and my toe was just able to reach.

By the time I got home, limp-waddled my packages inside, wrapped them and got dressed in a large red muumuu, I was already forty-five minutes late for the party and very frustrated. I just wasn't used to this. I was an athlete, a Rhodes Scholar, and a White House official. But none of that mattered. I put in all the effort of a champion and still failed.

Several weeks before Darcy was born, Grant and I sat in easy chairs in front of the fireplace in our living room.

Whenever I sat still she would begin to move, kick, and turn around inside me. It was like watching an earthquake on my belly. I used to worry that something was wrong. After she was born I learned: she just liked to move!

We watched my tummy for a while, then I asked, "Tell me a story?" One of the reasons that I wanted to marry Grant was that he told me stories, usually about an unlikely hero who gathers a rag-tag gang together for a series of dangerous adventures.

"What kind of story?" he asked.

"A story about you, me, and the baby. Actually, what I really want are pictures. When I try to imagine us doing things together, I can't. I have no pictures in my head." I guessed that other mothers had happy images in their heads to look forward to, but I suddenly realized I had none. Not one. I didn't know why.

I knew I wasn't a very maternal woman. I never enjoyed shopping, gossiping, and soap operas. I just thought I wasn't very girlie. It never bothered me, until then, when I was pregnant.

So Grant "told" me pictures: playing guitar, going to the beach, laughing together. I tried to see myself in those pictures. I felt a little better.

My water broke at 3:00 a.m., but there were no contractions yet. Grant called the doctor on duty, who suggested we go back to sleep—we'd need it for the long ordeal of delivery. At 4:00 a.m. the contractions started. We were slowly getting ready, gathering up things to do during the long period of labor we anticipated in the hospital.

As Grant timed the next set of contractions he got a funny look in his eyes.

"I think we need to go. *Now!*" The contractions were already only five minutes apart. We stopped packing and got into our little red Escort. I couldn't sit down because of the pain. I got on my knees, facing backward, and grabbed the passenger seat headrest while Grant drove.

At the hospital, nurses began checking me in at a normal pace, which felt very slow to me, since the contractions hurt so much.

"If I have to do this for eighteen hours," I thought, "I am definitely getting an epidural!"

As soon as I got on the table and was examined, people stopped moving slowly.

"Get her doctor in here. *Now!*" said the nurse. "She's at nine centimeters!"

"Epidural?" I asked as soon as I could speak.

"Oh, no," said the nurse. "By the time it kicked in, the baby would be here already. It's too late for an epidural." Grant says I tried to rip all the hair off his chest.

We left the house at 4:00 a.m. By 6:00 a.m., Darcy Sinclair Deane had arrived. What a beauty! She looked at us with all-knowing eyes. Her features were so delicate, like rosebuds. She had an elegant way of holding her hands.

I felt anxious when they took her away for a blood test and weighing. When they brought her back and placed her on my breast I could relax and rest. She calmed me.

Marty Evans

Marsha, or "Marty" Evans, is one of only a handful of women ever to attain the honored rank of rear admiral in the navy. After retiring in 1998, she was asked to lead the Girl Scouts of the USA, the largest organization for girls in the world. From there, she went on to head the Red Cross, where she served as president and CEO until 2005.

She is tall, fit, and attractive in a wholesome, girl-next-door kind of way. She is known to be a strong leader, but also a fun person. It's not unusual to see her on the dance floor with young people at the various youth events where she appears.

When she was promoted to an admiral in the navy in the 1990s, it happened to be just after the Tailhook scandal. For her first acting duty as an admiral, she was named to head a special task force created to change the culture and climate of the navy to respect women.

The scandal began when it became public that the navy's Tailhook Convention included many cases of harassing and molesting of women. Things got worse when the Pentagon reported that senior navy officials deliberately undermined their own investigation to avoid bad publicity and ignored the participation of senior officers at Tailhook. President Bill Clinton fired the secretary of the navy and Marty was the woman who was supposed to figure out what to do.

As a brand new admiral, this was her first assignment. For Marty the task felt enormous—overwhelming. The Tailhook scandal was in the media every day, and she was on the hot seat. The scariest thing of all was that it looked like she probably would fail this challenge. In her twenty-four years in the navy she had always gotten things done well.

But Marty was the scapegoat—set up with an impossible task—and expected to fail. She was the woman who would take the blame for the navy's treatment of women when the next crisis emerged. No one expected her to turn the ship.

Marty thought to herself "Why me?" She hadn't asked for this. She was a good officer and could have done so many other things with her skills. She wondered, "What if I just can't do this?"

I remember one crisp October day when I walked into my office at the Pentagon. The office had an exterior view, which was pretty special in the Pentagon. I walked over to the blackboard and picked up a piece of chalk. It was an old-fashioned blackboard on a big oak stand, the kind where the board rotated so you could write on both sides. I started writing, and the entire framework for a solution came flowing out of my chalk.

The framework I wrote became the basis for changing the law to allow women in combat roles. Today the treatment of women is significantly better: you don't mistreat the members of your team who you rely on with your life. It had an influence that was felt far and wide outside the military as well.

It was the answer to several days of particularly intense prayer. What was remarkable to me was how fully formed the ideas came out. Suddenly, the whole thing seemed simple.

I asked myself, "Why are women being attacked, denigrated, and disrespected?" The navy had a law that prevented women from doing many of the jobs they were qualified to do. Suddenly it came to me, since women were not allowed to be on the team and to go into combat, they were not respected.

You can't imagine how hard I prayed through the entire Tailhook experience. When I learned how to pray way back in Sunday school, we were told that you can't just go right into asking for the forty-two things you want. I learned to pray with the acronym ACTS: adoration, confession, thanksgiving, and supplication. That means before you get to supplication, you have to adore God, confess your sins, and give thanks.

But as I led the Task Force, my supplication was way out of balance. I found myself asking for a lot. I really did need help. I didn't know where to start. There was no book, no manual, and no leadership guide to cover this unique situation. I was challenged to my limits. I prayed hard from August to October.

The experience changed me. I learned two things. First, it's a fact that God never gives you more of a burden than you can bear. I had heard those words before, but after that experience I knew it as a fact. Even if your burden may seem too heavy, you'll be given the strength you need to get through.

Second, I learned that life's burdens make us more grateful. I am a Christian, but I learned the Buddhist perspective: the times we have burdens are necessary to make us appreciate the times without burdens.

I have always prayed regularly, but my prayer routine has changed as more pressures crowd out the meditative quality of my prayer. I increasingly need to rejuvenate or restart myself. I need blank space. Regular exercise is the one time when I really do have some success in tuning everything out and getting a mental break.

I find myself praying as I dress after working out in the gym. I go to a gym with very few women. In the locker room I am alone. It's peaceful.

It's a ritual for me. I clear my mind and I pray. If I try to start solving problems too quickly, I mess up the ritual and it doesn't work.

One of my problems is "owning" more issues than I should. Because I came from an alcoholic family, I grew up feeling that if only I could achieve enough I could somehow fix my father.

It's a common problem. In my case, I became hyper-responsible for everything. It's a struggle for me to let go and let others own part of a problem. As a leader it is better for me to tackle the largest, most complex problems and leave the rest to others. But, truth be known, I love the little details. I struggle to step back, see the big picture, and be more strategic.

I think prayer helps me to be a better leader. After consciously clearing my mind, I can see things differently. I am better, not only in my job, but also in my personal relationships. Creating a blank space for forty-five minutes without worrying and having intrusive thoughts allows me to pray on the right things. I can skip one day, but if I skip two, I get more obsessive.

When I pray I reflect on my imperfections. I ask God to perfect the imperfections in me. Organizations reflect the behavior, values and attitude of their leader. As a leader, you get back what you reflect.

So I pray for things like:

Make me the person that others will want to follow.
Make me a good reflection and a model of the best qualities.
Help eliminate the flaws in the mirror.
Make my actions and values—both conscious and unconscious—worthy of imitation.

Line Dancing with Jesus

BONNIE'S STORY

I took a deep breath, shut the door of my hotel room, headed toward the elevator, and went down to the conference center adjacent to the hotel.

As I walked I went through a mental checklist: I'm wearing my red, white, and blue Olympic jacket, my Olympic medals, shorts, and sneakers; hair done; makeup done. I began reviewing the speech in my head for the hundredth time.

I had left my job at the White House to start a family with my husband and to become a speaker and author. Having a child and wanting to be at home gave me the courage to follow my dream of inspiring others as a writer and speaker. Telling the story of the one-legged girl from San Diego who becomes a ski racer was something only I could do.

In the two years since I'd left Washington, I was very productive on the home front: our daughter Darcy was one year old. In terms of writing, I had successfully landed a contract for my first book. Developing my reputation as a speaker, however, had proven more difficult than I'd thought.

Even though I had many achievements—ski medals, White House experience—no one wanted to hire me to speak for a big convention unless I could prove I had done it before. I was getting little jobs, speaking for fifty people, one hundred people, and once even one thousand people. I also spoke at a number of big conventions for free—not as the headliner but as one of many presenters for small workshops. I was building my experience and skill as a speaker, but it was slow and hard work.

Grant and I struggled to make ends meet. With a new baby, our expenses were up while money was down with only one salary. Our time, energy, and patience were stretched as tight as our wallets.

As I walked toward the convention center I could feel tension washing throughout my body. This time I was the headliner!

Today I would be keynote speaker for a conference of more than 10,000 people from around the world. My biggest fear was that I would pee in my pants when I got on stage. I was afraid I would stand there and forget my lines, like I did in the church pageant so many years ago.

I went into the meeting room. Holy-moley! It was as big as a football field. The ceiling was so high you almost felt outdoors. I began walking from the back through the dark sea of empty chairs toward the dramatically lit stage. I felt dwarfed.

When I reached the stage I introduced myself to the producer in charge. He brought over the sound tech, who put on my microphone and sent me on stage to test it. When I finished the mic check, I asked, "Where's the bathroom?"

When I gave speeches, I needed quiet time where I could close my eyes. In a crowded convention center, the bathroom was the only place. I shut myself into a stall, sat down and began my ritual of focus to do my best. I used the same mental focus technique that had worked for ski races.

I was terrified. This felt more frightening than exams at Harvard or even racing at the Olympics. At least in skiing and school I felt like I knew what I was doing. I wasn't sure what 10,000 human resource professionals wanted me to say. As I sat there, tense and afraid, trying to go through the steps to focus my mind, suddenly an image of Jesus intruded into my thoughts.

It wasn't just the face of Jesus, it was His whole body. And He wasn't just standing there, He was . . . He was line dancing?!?!!

As I sat there in the bathroom stall at the convention center, I saw myself line dancing to the country and western Muzak playing through the hotel's sound system. Jesus was kicking up His sandals; His robes were flying as we danced. He smiled at me and His blue eyes laughed.

All my tension melted away. I laughed and relaxed. I felt He came to help me and He gave me exactly what I needed. It was especially striking because I had not thought about Jesus in years.

I went out on stage with confidence and joy. I gave the speech of my life.

As a result, many of the corporations in the audience hired me to speak for years afterward. I used a recorded tape of that speech as my demo for prospective clients. In so many ways, that speech kicked off my current career working as a headliner for major conferences and Fortune 500 clients all over the country. Thank You, Jesus!

My experience of being supported by God through prayer in a critical work situation was similar to Marty Evans being supported by God at work. She, however, had prayed over many months and asked for help. I had been meditating for quite a while to prepare for speeches, but God reached out to me with my vision of Jesus . . . line dancing!

After that, I began to invite God into my mental preparation for speeches more and more. I had been making quiet time a priority and that is where God found me. By the end of one year, I felt that I worked with God and that God worked through me to inspire people.

To give speeches, I knew I needed God's help. Oddly enough though, I didn't feel I needed God's help in my private life. We struggled with parenting, marriage, and daily life without any thought that God could help. We believed in God, but didn't understand that He could make a difference on a daily basis. That seems incredible to me now, looking back.

For the next two years, my relationship with God grew and grew. But it was strictly a work-based relationship.

Amy Grant

Singer and songwriter Amy Grant lives in Nashville, Tennessee, with her GRAMMY Award-winning country singer husband Vince Gill and their blended family of five children. The pretty brunette with the infectious smile has won numerous accolades for her music. The Dove Award for contemporary album of the year and Artist of the Year, and the GRAMMY Award for best gospel performance. She was the first artist to perform a Christian music song for a GRAMMY broadcast. Her song "Baby, Baby" was the first pop song by a Christian artist to reach the coveted number one spot on *Billboard*'s chart.

Amy started writing songs when she was just fifteen. Actively involved in a youth group at a hippy church down on Music Row in Nashville, a lot of the groups' kids lived in public housing. There were drug problems and teen pregnancies during the time she was involved with the group. It was a very different world from where Amy went to school.

She describes her father, a doctor, as a very gentle, quiet

man. She was well taken care of and went to a fine girls' school. Amy was drawn to this church "because, there, I felt like all the Bible teaching I had in my very sheltered world just came face-to-face with people having real-life problems," she says.

When she first started writing songs, Amy would sing them for the kids in the youth group at this church. One day, one of the kids said to her "I just get this feeling when you start singing, Amy, that if you would just let God, that He would use you." Amy remembers kneeling down in that circle of kids and asking them "Would you guys pray for me? Pray that whatever God wants to happen in my life I won't get in the way."

That prayer in her teens with the hippy church youth group set her mind in a new way. Rather than wanting to be a star, Amy wanted to feel a sense of purpose with her music. She was willing to let God use her to spread His Word.

She feels what's happened to her career-wise was like the little boy who showed up with five loaves and two fish. You know the story: Jesus prayed and it turned into enough to feed 5,000 with baskets of food left over!

Nowadays, I do pray, but it's not at a specific time with a specific posture. I don't know that I have very many routines in my life period.

The first thing I see in the morning, with my eyes blurry before I put my contacts in, is the coffee pot. The best sound I hear in the morning is the hiss when the water runs all the way through the steamer. My mind is always really fuzzy in the morning so I don't always wake up thinking "Thank You, God, for this day, it's good to be alive."

There have been times in my life when I have been so scattered—running and answering calls and driving carpool—that I would get hours into a day and say: Gosh, I have not even turned my attention on the One who made me! I haven't even prayed for my children yet!

Then one day I found myself in a hole-in-the-wall craft store in Colorado where I saw a charm made of twisted wire wrapped around several objects. As soon as I saw it I thought to myself: This is the answer to my morning! I was determined to use this charm to start the day off right.

So I bought that charm and hung it by the coffee pot on a cabinet knob! When I see it, I say "Oh, right!" and I pray, "God, create in me a clean heart. If your mercies are new every morning, and I believe they are, I need new mercies for this day, and make me right with You so that I can be right with other people."

I have assigned different meanings to each of the things wrapped in the wire, kind of like a hippy rosary, I guess. At the top of the stack is a pale stone heart—that reminds me to pray for a clean heart. Then you go on down and there's a little ivory flower—there I pray for our home to be a safe and loving place where we can all grow. Below that there's a ring with hearts on it, where I pray for my relationship with Vince to be strong and full of love. And at the very end is a little keychain with little miniature keys, which reminds me to pray for each of my kids. I don't have a set thing that I say, but I just tick down the wire.

That might seem really goofy for some people, but I have kind of a "milkweed in the wind" personality. Whatever Type A is . . . I'm definitely not that.

My favorite place to pray is outside, partly because it's away from anything man-made . . . away from the clutter of my own life and my to-do list.

If I can just walk outside, I say: Oh, yeah, that tree God made, that sunset, those clouds rushing overhead, the birds in the air. I'm reminded of Scripture: "He knows when a sparrow falls, He knows every hair on your head" (see Matthew 10:29-30).

There are times that I have just danced with joy under a full moon, arms flung out to the stars, just dancing . . . so glad that nobody could see me, but wanting to say without words: "God, this is how I feel about all the great things that I've experienced in this life. I was running and jumping and twirling!" And that is a form of prayer.

Singing can be prayer for me, too. That verse comes to mind, Acts 17:28: "For in him we live and move and have our being" (KJV). So where does prayer stop and start? I know there are times that we're consciously in prayer, especially when we're in need: "Thanks God, I don't know what to do here. Please inspire me. Give me the words to say." That obviously is active praying.

But I think there are times when you see a sunset and it catches your breath. The sky goes from pink to lavender to deep purple and your eyes well up with tears and all you're doing is just chill bumping. I think that's worship, when you acknowledge: "God, You did a great thing when You made this world!"

When I heard about this book, *How Strong Women Pray*, what came to my mind was: strong or stubborn? Strong women can take on everything and try to solve everything. We don't always accept help graciously.

But prayer instantly reorients the frazzled mind. To humble yourself enough to bow your head says, "God, I know You see the whole picture." It puts things in their proper place; that's what prayer does. Whatever view I have is limited by where I am on the continent, where I am in my period cycle, where I am in my life, where I am emotionally. But when you start praying, when you address God, suddenly you're talking to the One who sees it all. Along with that, trust replaces worry.

One night, Vince and I were lying in bed and I said "I just cannot sleep. Can we pray together for the kids?" I had a son and two daughters, Vince had one daughter, and together we had another daughter.

My prayer was simple. We mentioned each one by name and what was going on with them from my perspective. Then, of course, I'm reminded: "God, You see this child. You see this teenager. You created them and You know all their green light zones. You know the things that are going to give them a sense of purpose." When I prayed, I felt my heart stop racing. Praying gave me peace.

The most important thing I've learned about prayer is in my failures. I have learned how deep and wide and high and long the love of Christ is. In the ways that I've let myself down or let other people down, I've realized the absolute healing power of forgiveness.

In Sunday school class we were studying about the life of Peter. Somebody asked, What is the difference between Peter and Judas? As a young child, I would have said, "Judas was a scoundrel who betrayed Jesus."

But what's the difference between the guy that betrayed Him and wound up killing himself and the guy that betrayed Jesus and wound up being the rock on which the church was built? The only difference between those two is that one felt that his sin was too great to be forgiven and the other trusted absolutely the power of love and forgiveness.

God can and does forgive anything. The difference is not what Judas did wrong. It's that Judas gave up. He felt like he had done the unforgivable. But according to Jesus, there is no unforgivable. There's nothing that can separate us from Him, nothing.

"For I am convinced that neither death nor life, neither angels nor demons, neither the present nor the future, nor any powers, neither height nor depth, nor anything else in all creation, will be able to separate us from the love of God that is in Christ Jesus our Lord" (Romans 8:38-39 NIV).

One of the gifts of being forty-five is that I really know that at a gut level. I know that as a result of countless snot cries with my face in the dirt! Times when I have messed up so bad that I know I am so far beyond dropping the ball; I am at real failure. Nobody wants to be there. But that's really where you find Jesus. You find Him in other ways at other times, but He shines the brightest when you think there's no hope.

There's a Bible verse in Hebrews that says, because we have Jesus who knows every temptation that we've known, "Let us hold fast the confession of our hope without wavering, for He who promised is faithful" (Hebrews 10:23 NKJV).

I always think about that verse and say, "Do not be afraid to bow your head because there's not anything that you can think or do that is going to be a shock to God."

Letting God Work Through Me

Bonnie's Story

After the flurry of packing my clothes, taking care of last minute things and making sure that Grant and Darcy would be okay for a day or two, it was a relief to get through airport security, get onto the plane, and fasten my seat belt.

During the flight all I could do was relax. It was the bridge between the hectic life of a working mother and the intensity of standing up in front of hundreds or thousands to give a speech. I did this a few times each month.

To prepare, I always learned as much as possible about the audience. Before leaving home I interviewed people on the phone to better understand their challenges, frustrations, and opportunities to excel. Once I arrived on site, I connected with people and picked their brains. If there was a cocktail party or dinner, I attended it and mingled with a mission. If no event was held, I often approached attendees in the hotel lobby, bar, or restaurant. I made friends easily.

But here, sitting on the plane was not the time to get

more information. I closed my eyes and enjoyed the opportunity to pray without the interruption of phones, mail, chores, and other demands. Looking out the window and seeing myself amid the fluffy clouds high in the blue sky, I felt close to God.

I let my mind quiet down, sometimes with visualization, like walking to the edge of a jetty toward a river or sitting on a cloud. Once I felt calm, I said to myself "This is Your speech God, not mine. I know that You have already written a nourishing, inspiring speech just for this particular group. Please show me what this speech is about . . . what You want to do with it."

Sometimes I would get a clear sense right away. A topic like, "The Power of Personal Vision," or "Choosing to Be Extraordinary," might come to mind, along with certain stories from my life and stories I had heard in my pre-interviews. I would know the core feeling I needed to convey to strengthen them. It felt good.

Sometimes, though, I would not immediately get a clear sense of what the speech should be about. At first that worried me. The time to give the speech would get closer and closer but I wouldn't have a clear, gut sense of what the speech should be about.

Over time I learned to let go and trust God. So often there was a person I needed to meet or a story I needed to hear before I could get that sense of the core meaning of the speech. A few times it just came through while I spoke . . . that requires total trust. To walk on stage trusting completely that the right words will be there for me is like falling backward into the arms of God without questioning that you will be caught. That is a glorious feeling.

Other times, though, I fought against trusting. I would get a sense of what I needed to say and then push back. "I can't give *that* speech!" Once I was speaking for a paper company and fought against it so hard, that minutes before walking on stage I had two entirely different speeches in my head. One was tamer and more socially acceptable. The other was a bit more challenging for the audience, pushing them to stop feeling sorry for themselves and do what they would need to do to make their company competitive again.

I tried so hard to stick with the speech that was "nice." But when my mouth opened, the speech came out that was far more motivating. It was a big hit. What a relief!

One day, in the middle of winter, I stood at the front end of a Veterans of Foreign War meeting hall in a small midwestern town, listening to the announcements at a spaghetti dinner, auction, and fundraiser for the girls' high-school basketball team. I was due to give a keynote speech in a few minutes.

I smiled, took the mike, stepped onto a chair, and then walked up on top of the table at the front of the room. There was no stage, so I just stood on the table.

I certainly got the attention of everyone in the room. When I finished, I stepped down off the table.

So many times I have stood on a table to give a speech! Usually it is at community events where they don't have proper staging.

Always, in the moment before I step onto a table, I feel a strong desire not to do it. All kinds of thoughts run through my head:

"They will think you are crazy."

"They will think you are full of yourself."

"What if the table collapses?"

"It's the fault of the organizers for not having a stage; it's not your fault that you're short."

I can find a hundred reasons not to get up on that table. There is no doubt in my mind that I would be more comfortable staying on the floor. So what makes me do it?

The reason is simple: I believe God works through me when I give speeches and I want to do my absolute best. There is an energy that comes through me from God that is delivered to the audience. There shouldn't be anything between us. I don't stand behind podiums. I want to get myself enough out of the way so that the Light can shine through. Letting the Light shine through me is what I pray for before I speak. I cannot give less than everything, so I must find the courage to get on that table, and shine with all my heart.

As women, I think we often believe we have fewer ego problems because we hang back more instead of putting ourselves forward. But it is important to understand that hanging back can be just as much of an ego problem. For me, not standing on the table would be putting myself and my comfort ahead of serving others. It is like Amy Grant's prayer: "God, don't let me get in the way!"

Ego would tell me not to risk having others think I am odd or full of myself.

But God made me to inspire others and He gives me the courage to do it.

Martha Williamson

Martha Williamson was the first female executive producer of two television shows at once. Best known for *Touched by an Angel,* a top ten hit that stayed on the air for nine years and spun-off *The Promised Land,* which ran for three seasons. Because 99 percent of shows get cancelled in the first season, this was an amazing achievement.

But Martha initially turned down the chance to produce *Touched by an Angel.*

She was producing a pilot for CBS with Thomas Carter called *Under One Roof.* Martha thought it was groundbreaking television and was very proud to be a part of it. The pilot starred James Earl Jones, Joe Morton and Isabelle Callaway—all amazing actors. Her team turned in what she believed to be a wonderful pilot.

But on a Wednesday morning in May, she and Thomas got the call that *Under One Roof* was not picked up. To make matters worse, the network had picked up a show that Martha had heard on the street was a "piece of junk" called *Angel's Attic.* Thomas and Martha were furious. They saw the rejection as some kind of a racial statement.

Martha was in shock. She could not believe that CBS had not picked up her show. She was angry. Not necessarily the best time to make any decisions, especially important decisions.

Later that day, her agent called and said, "They have another show they want you to look at called *Angel's Attic*. But they have just renamed it. They are going to call it *Touched by an Angel*."

"Oh, that's so much better!" she said to her agent sarcastically as she rolled her eyes. The network sent over a video for her to look at right away. That very afternoon, while she was still steaming from the rejection, Martha put in the videotape and watched in horror. It was everything that Christians don't like about television.

Martha recalls the first thirty seconds of the video. Monica dive-bombed out of the atmosphere into the ocean, then she poped up out of the ocean, walked onto the shore and made a joke with a couple of stoned druggies and found her way to Della Reese's house. Della's character smoked, drank, swore, and was sarcastic.

"These are supposed to be angels?" Martha thought. It only got worse. Her spirit was so offended that she turned it off, picked up the phone, and indignantly told her agent, "I wouldn't touch this with a ten-foot pole." She turned it down.

Martha thought she was being a wonderful Christian by refusing to be involved in something she found so offensive to her faith. But she had not prayed about it.

How many times have I found myself in a pickle and then suddenly realized I had not prayed about my circumstances? Why is this the last thing we think of instead of the first thing?

So often we will forget to pray . . . but we haven't forgotten God. It is simply that we have used our own understanding as a replacement for prayer. We have leaned on our own understanding and, frankly, our ego.

But by not praying about *Touched by an Angel*, I did not give God the opportunity to show me all the possibilities. I rejected the idea of working on the show on a Wednesday. By Friday, I realized that in every prayer I had prayed since Wednesday, God continued to impress the angel show on my heart.

Everything in my head was saying "No way, no way." But when I prayed, I got this awareness and I thought "God, you have got to be kidding me."

That is also when you realize finally that prayer is truly a two-way street. When you don't listen, it is like picking up the phone and talking and hanging up before anyone has the chance to respond.

I have finally learned to recognize the difference between what I put into my head and what God puts into my heart. I discover something present in my spirit that made itself known to me without any thought process.

I didn't *get there* to that thought or that idea, I discovered it. Then I prayed about it and asked for God's confirmation. I realized "Oh . . . yes, this is something the Lord has put there and it is true." In this case, that angel show kept coming back to my heart.

Now, at the same time, I was offered a job on a different show with big stars on another network and I was going to get more money than I had ever received before. I had to accept or reject the job by Friday night. But I knew that I was supposed to do that angel show.

I called my agent. I said, "You are going to think I am crazy, but I think I want to go back and do the angel show."

And she said, "I think it is too late."

She called and the network said, "We are going to interview somebody else who is coming in from New York next Tuesday, so you can come back in and interview next Wednesday."

I realized that I was in big trouble. If I accepted the other job, which was a sure thing at the time, I would lose the job God wanted me to have. But if I was wrong, I could end up with no job. The way show business works is there is a huge scramble to staff all the shows in a very short period of time. It's like musical chairs. If you don't find yourself a seat very quickly, you could end up out of the game for a year or longer.

So basically I had the angel show offered to me and turned it down cold. Now, to get it back I would have to turn down a fabulous offer and then interview against others.

I called a friend and I asked, "Will you pray with me?" We prayed and felt God saying I was supposed to say no to this other job and trust Him. So I did. I spent a very long weekend. . . . Oh, boy!

I walked back in to CBS on Wednesday and I remember sitting in that third floor lobby where everybody sits while they are waiting to go in and see the executives. I'd sat there many, many, many times for one reason or another, but I will never forget sitting there that day. Once again, the Lord impressed on my heart a Scripture: "The LORD is my light and my salvation—whom shall I fear?" (Psalm 27:1 NIV). I knew that He was already in the room.

I walked into that room with the president of CBS, the executive vice president of CBS, all the other network development executives, and the head of drama, and they all looked at me. I walked in and I sat down and said, "I do know how to do this show. I didn't know last week, but I know how to do it now."

I told them that the only way they could get an audience for a show about angels is to get people who believe in angels and like angels to watch it. "You can't turn around and offend the very people you are trying to attract," I explained. I told them to throw the pilot out and start over.

Every show has to have rules. You're creating a whole universe just the way *Star Trek* created its universe. It had a prime directive that you don't break and this show needed to have a prime directive, too.

But one of the executives objected, "We have to be up and running with this show. We are so far behind. You'll need time to develop those rules."

I insisted that I didn't need more time. "The rules are already written," I told them. "They are right here . . . in the Bible."

They gave me permission to do anything I wanted to do, and that included recasting. I explained that the only thing that I would keep about the show would be Roma Downey and Della Reese. I would start all over with everything else. They basically threw a $2 million pilot away and let me start over.

The prime directive for *Touched by an Angel* was simple. God exists. God loves you and God wants to be part of your life. That is what Roma or Della always explained to the main character in every show.

The original pilot had Roma Downey flying all the time. Whenever she raised her arms, it looked like she had Venetian blinds coming down underneath. It was horrible. I told them firmly, "No flying, no swearing and no drinking."

I told the executives to just imagine all those people out there who really want to see their faith reflected in a television show. Our team actually started using the phrase "people of faith" before it became an everyday phrase.

Using the term "people of faith" rather than "religious people" made it more accessible to CBS. People of faith want to see themselves reflected on television, too. But all you ever saw up until that point were negative images. If people were "religious" they were fanatics. They were intolerant. They were the mentally disturbed, axe-murdering parents of the troubled child. That is the way "religious people," people who believed in God, were always depicted on television . . . as extreme nuts. *Touched by an Angel* was a real breakthrough in showing people of faith in a positive light.

I have a regular prayer routine. Every morning, my husband, Jon Andersen, and I try very hard to pray together. When we got married eight years ago, we committed to pray every morning before we got out of bed. Now we have two little girls and our morning prayer has translated into what we call our "happy morning prayer" because the little ones now get up before we do and wake us up.

As a family we lay out for the Lord the way we hope the day will go and ask Him to bless that. In the evening, when we all get back together for dinner—and we always make it a point to have dinner together—we acknowledge in our dinner prayers the petitions that were answered that day.

This is incredibly important because, how many times do we pray and everything goes fine, and then we forget that God answered our prayer? We forget to give Him the glory. That is one of the great joys I have found: the more frequently we recognize the prayers that have been answered, the stronger our faith grows.

Because I am an older mom with tiny little children, I am

having a hard time going through kindergarten and meno-pause simultaneously. I find that I lose everything: my keys, my purse, you name it. Things are constantly misplaced and I am always praying to the Lord to help me remember what I did with them. It sounds so silly, but you know how one thing like that can turn into a big deal. Sometimes it's hard to be peaceful while getting little kids out the door. So I simply say, "Lord, it is in Your hands. Lord, You know where my keys are. I don't." I try to be at peace, knowing that maybe if I had my car keys, and if I were in my car right now, who knows whether somebody would run a red light and smack us?

When you are doing a network television show, just about every time the phone rings your heart leaps, the adrenaline surges through your body, and you know something bad is about to happen or has already happened . . . and now you have to fix it.

There is always something: a camera truck had just blown up from a propane accident; the actress's hair turned blue; or the dog won't bark on cue. Something is going to mess up your day.

So I got into the habit of what I call "Job-ing it," as in the Book of Job in the Bible. Every time something terrible happened to Job, he got on his knees and thanked God for it because you don't know what greater disaster you missed instead. I do that.

When I became a Christian at about age twenty-five, one of my best friends was horrified. He assumed that I was now going to become a person whose ideas were utterly opposite to who I had been before.

In a way, I was afraid of the same thing. I remember that after I accepted Jesus as my savior and asked Him into my heart, I stayed in bed the next morning because I was terrified I wouldn't be able to live up to what I had just committed to do. I didn't know how to be a Christian. I was going to have to be perfect now and I knew I couldn't do that. And I was afraid that God would ask me to do something that I didn't want to do.

Was I going to have to give up my dreams of being a television producer and go become a missionary in South America? I was so afraid that by turning my life over to God, He was going to turn my life upside down and make me miserable.

I was afraid to really follow God. And once I got to that point, I realized I was not pursuing with a whole heart and with great confidence the career that I wanted because I was afraid that I was doing something God didn't want me to do. So it wasn't until I turned it all over, laid it down at the altar, and resisted every temptation to run back to the altar and take it back, that I felt at peace.

And that means you have to be willing to give it all up. You have to say and believe that your career, your relationship, your image isn't more important than your relationship with God.

I got down on my knees and started to pray. I realized that even being on my knees wasn't enough. I had just seen *The Thorn Birds*, and I had seen Richard Chamberlain when he was being confirmed as a priest in Rome. He was flat on his face with his arms outstretched on the floor in front of the Pope. I thought "That's pretty humbling. How much more can one humble one's self?"

So I did it. I put myself flat on the floor and I put my nose to the carpet and something came over me. I saw there was still so much pride. I lay on that floor until I felt in every bone of my body how completely reliant I was on the Lord to guide me and sustain me.

I also realized at that moment how much I wanted to achieve my potential and how frightened I was at my very core that, if I did not, my life would have no meaning. I stayed on that floor until I could completely say to the Lord with whole heart and, as it says in the Bible: "The sacrifices of God are a broken spirit; a broken and contrite heart" (Psalm 51:17 NIV). I struggled for complete commitment to put myself under God's authority and to put my career entirely in His hands.

I said to God, "From now on, I am not going to worry about it. I'm going to take everything day by day. I'm going to trust You to inform me which things are opportunities and which are liabilities, but I am never going to worry about my career again." And I never did.

From that day on, once I turned the worry over to Him, my prayers were no longer requests for anything, but guidance and intuition. I didn't say, "I really need this job," "I want to be this," or "I want to meet this person." I simply said, "Lord, what do You have for me today? Should I turn left or should I turn right? Should I make this call? Should I write this?" I was constantly tuning and attuning myself to the voice of the Holy Spirit.

Lately I've realized that I need to go through that process and surrender myself again. I need to say, "Lord, forgive me, because I think I have run back to the altar recently and dragged my career off. It's not my career, God. It is Your career." Sometimes we have to pray again the same prayer and relearn the same things again and again.

PART V

IN THE VALLEY, WE GROW

On Top of the World

I walked onto the set for NBC's *Today Show* for my guest appearance as a woman who had everything. I wore a red, white, and blue Olympic jacket with my silver and two bronze medals around my neck. I wore shorts to show off my blue, titanium sports leg.

Matt Lauer sat with me on the sofa and asked about each of my achievements: Rhodes scholarship, Harvard degree, White House economic official and, of course, the ski racing. He asked about my husband, Grant, and my three-year-old daughter, Darcy. Under the hot studio lights, I basked in the glow of having it all. As a motivational speaker, I worked from home and had time to spend with my daughter, but also enjoyed the feeling that I was making the world a better place. I had worked and struggled to create a life for myself that included everything I thought I needed to be happy. The five-minute interview ended in what felt like the blink of an eye.

Montel Williams saw me on the *Today Show* and decided to

devote an entire hour of his TV show to my story . . . something he had only done for six people before. Nine million viewers would hear about my story and about my first book, *Succeeding Sane*.

A tremendous opportunity with only one catch: He wanted to focus on the sexual abuse in my childhood. Since I had never talked about it before in public, I wasn't sure what to do. To make me more comfortable, the *Montel Show* sent tapes of similar shows so that I could see that the show would be tastefully done.

The taping was supposed to start in forty-eight hours. A flurry of emotions, phone calls, and arrangements began. Decisions had to be made quickly. Some were easy: Grant and I decided our daughter was not going to appear on a show that focused on abuse. Non-negotiable. Grant, however, decided he would go on the air and be interviewed in order to support me.

Other decisions were harder. The producers asked my mother to appear on the show. I was worried they would try to blame her for what had happened. I knew they would ask all kinds of questions trying to find out one thing: How could you not know what was going on?

My stepfather started his sick hobby with both my sister and me shortly after marrying my mother. I was only two years old and my sister, five. Because he was retired and my mother worked until after 5 p.m., he had free access to us after school before she came home. He stopped molesting my sister when she was six, probably because she was becoming more likely to tell. He didn't leave me alone, though, until four years later when I turned seven. Perhaps he had a harder time stopping with me because there wasn't another girl waiting in line.

Although I had faced steep ski slopes and audiences of 10,000 people, I had never faced up to my feelings about childhood abuse. All of my life I coped with my past by avoiding thinking about it. From the very beginning, my denial was so deep that my brain actually blocked the memories until my stepfather died when I was eighteen. After I remembered, I coped by moving on with my life, just like my mother told me to do.

My sister, on the other hand, coped by expressing her pain and getting help. Besides the support of her close girlfriends, she joined several support groups and went to a therapist. She had encouraged me to do the same, but I waved it away.

"Heck," I thought, "I'm an Olympic ski medalist, Rhodes Scholar, author, and businesswoman. Nothing's wrong with me!"

As the furious preparation for the *Montel Show* began, I called my mother to discuss it. Normally, we all avoided this subject because it was so painful. I had no idea what she thought.

"Mom, they are going to ask you on the show when you first found out about the abuse. What will you say?"

"When I read your book," she answered, as if the answer was perfectly obvious, "*Succeeding Sane.*"

I was shocked. I knew I had told her about it when I was eighteen. I had mentioned it on several occasions since. I knew my sister had mentioned it more often than I did. Now my mother was saying she only found out this year. How could she "forget" all the other times she heard about it?

My mother, who also had been sexually abused as a child, coped, not just by "putting it behind her," but by dissociating or blanking out her abuse memories—and ours—to avoid the pain. I felt sorry for her. I didn't want her to go on the show. They would tear her to pieces. I got the producers to agree to do the show without her.

Grant and I flew to New York and were greeted with a limo to take us to the hotel. In the morning, Grant rushed with me to Lord and Taylor as soon as it opened to find something suitable for me to wear. In fifteen minutes we found a peach silk suit that fit and then raced over to the studio. I turned myself over to the makeup and hair people. I worried constantly about whether I was making a big mistake. Grant was a rock through everything.

As the moment got closer to stepping out on stage, I was a wreck. I could hear the live audience murmuring like an ocean on the other side of the curtain. As my fear rose up higher and higher I found myself repeating Psalm 23 . . . Yea, though I walk through the valley of the shadow of death, I will fear no evil (KJV). It was as though talking about my stepfather, Paul, would somehow make me a helpless, terrified child again.

Once the interview began, it got easier. Montel was kind. He continuously held up my book and encouraged people to buy it. On commercial breaks, he and his staff flipped through my book to reference their favorite parts. I was impressed by how much work they put into telling the story—the skiing, my disability, everything.

They brought out Barbara Warmath as a surprise guest. It was such a joy to see her after so many years! It was so nice of her to come out to support me on the show also.

The hardest thing was seeing this picture of Paul on the screen. They showed it over and over. It was Thanksgiving and he was standing over an enormous, shiny turkey that my mother had cooked. He had a big fork and knife ready to carve. He smiled broadly with the three of us kids around him. My mother must have been taking the picture. It made my stomach queasy every time I had to look at him, smiling.

Near the end of the show, when I realized I had talked about what happened without dying or being destroyed, I felt liberated! At the end of the show, I held up my fist and vowed to reclaim my feelings for myself. Little did I know where that journey would take me.

My sister warned me that talking about the abuse in public would have aftershocks and suggested I seek help. Again, I dismissed her advice. "My life is great," I thought. "Why do I need help?"

But she was right. I found it hard to "just put it behind me and get on with life." Our home, our daughter, and even my husband increasingly made me anxious.

Coming home from preschool with Darcy triggered my memories of being assaulted after preschool while my mother was still at work. The effort of suppressing the memories in that particular situation drained me so much that I fell asleep on the floor as Darcy played. I had no idea why. More often than not, I avoided being home in the afternoons by taking Darcy out to the mall until dinner.

My behavior was typical of people with PTSD (Post Traumatic Stress Disorder). I avoided and suppressed painful memories without even knowing I was doing it. It steadily took a toll on me. Since mothering was new to me, it was hard to know what was "normal stress" for a new mom and what was not. Like all new moms, I just coped the best I could.

Susan Taylor

Turn off that television!" Susan Taylor fussed at her daughter Nequai as she rushed around, pots and pans clanking, to make dinner. "Where is your homework? Did you clean up your room?"

As editorial director of *Essence* magazine, with more than 7.5 million readers, Susan had one of publishing's most high-powered and demanding jobs. For decades her profile has been the very logo for the magazine. She is an icon, tall and elegant, with long, svelte braids flowing down her back, embodying the beauty, the spirit, and the passion of women of color.

But the picture at home was different. Many days she arrived home from the office tired, completely anxious, and stressed out. Like mothers everywhere, she'd burst through the front door like a tornado, step out of her heels on the way to kitchen to start dinner, chopping, sautéing, and fussing all the while.

One evening, an out-of-town friend came home with her after work. After witnessing her madness, he asked, "Is that how you come home to Nequai every day?"

"The nerve!" Susan thought to herself. She gave that brother fever! "I am raising my daughter the way my parents raised me and I turned out fine, thank you!" She went on and on. But the truth was she heard him. She saw herself the way he saw her, and the way her daughter must see her, and she knew that it was time she made another choice.

Over time, she started coming home from work differently. Rather than bursting through the door as if the apartment were on fire, she'd stop and hug and kiss her darling daughter. Then, she'd excuse herself while she took a few minutes to restore herself. In their small, one-bedroom apartment, Susan would retreat to the quiet of the bathroom to sit still for a moment.

There, she would remind herself to leave the pressures of work at work and come back to her center. She'd remind herself not to scream and holler, but to be gentle and loving. Before cooking and correcting, she learned to just sit with Nequai for a few minutes and ask her about her day.

At first, her daughter found it strange that she was even interested. But soon she began to trust Susan's new behavior, and positive changes began to take place in their household. Perhaps for the first time, Susan felt happy and calm in the evening. She began to look forward to the time for nurturing and rekindling the love within her home. And Nequai grew calmer and happier, too. In time she went from being a failing student to an honor student, and eventually, the valedictorian of her class.*

This experience taught Susan so much about the importance of a connection to God, and has changed the way she approaches her life.

---

* *From* Lessons in Living *by Susan Taylor. New York: Anchor, 1998, pgs. 82-83. Used with permission from Random House.*

Today, I not only end my day differently but I also changed the way I begin it. After the alarm goes off, I stay in bed for an extra five minutes. I don't push the snooze alarm because that just creates more stress. I lie on my back and count the blessings I have in my life. I start every day with a smile on my face and a thankful heart. I affirm that I will not hassle, fuss, or bother. I affirm that I will take everything off my calendar that does not need to be there. Then, I get out of bed.

I spend about twenty minutes exercising. Either I run in Central Park or I go to the gym in my building. Sometimes I just march in place while I watch the news.

Next, I run a bath with aromatic herbs and bubbles. I light a candle. I soak for ten glorious minutes. By the time I get dressed and head for work, I am in the right frame of mind for a day of wonders.

I don't pray for miracles. I pray for the clarity to see my life as a most miraculous thing. I pray for the desire to love and to give more. These are the secret talismans that multiply our blessings. I make loving and giving my practice, and make that practice my prayer.

The changeless spiritual truth is this: God is absolute goodness. God is love, and love sustains and supplies everything it has created—the birds of the air, the lilies of the field, the light of the stars, and us. Because that's what love does—we don't have to earn it. That's what love is—giving and giving, unceasingly, unconditionally, without waiting for or wanting or needing thanks.

We are safe, even in the eye of the storm. God will never forsake us or take a break from blessing and loving us. Our prayers are for remembering that; for affirming it. Our prayers are for us. God doesn't need our prayers or praise. Nothing we can say or pray will make God love us more. As God's beloved, we have the divine right to live in all the many rooms of the mansion, the right to everything to fulfill your needs and obligations. Our prayers aren't for asking, but for affirming our faith—faith that we, as God's beloved, can be willing channels for the highest good, and that all our needs are met in the divine-right way, at the divine-right time.

Praising and thanking don't open God's heart wider. They open ours and fill it with love and gratitude, liberating us from fear, making us wiser, stronger.

If I had the chance to give advice to a younger person about prayer, I would tell them it's important to approach God from a place of abundance. Often we bargain with God or beg for what we believe we lack. But begging and pleading only affirm spiritual impoverishment and the belief in a God that withholds His grace and parcels it out for praise and flattery. This is the God of human invention—a jealous and vengeful God, in the image and likeness of what man has become. And this image of a bookkeeping, blessing-rationing, punishing God has been used to instill fear and limit our vision, even to justify our enslavement, demean women, and disempower our people.

Dr. Martin Luther King, Jr., said that the purpose of prayer is not to turn God into some cosmic bellhop we ring for whenever we want something. The purpose of prayer is to remind us of our oneness with God, that we are made in God's image, each of us a channel for divine influence, creativity, and power. With practice, prayer opens that channel. Prayer is more than praise and petition. It is about more than what we think or want. It's about selflessness, not self. It is not an insistence: "Listen, Holy Spirit, I am speaking," but rather, an invocation: "Speak, Holy Spirit, I am listening."

Beseeching God for blessings is like searching frantically for our glasses when they're sitting on our face. Our eyes are not the problem; it's our inner vision that's clouded. All life asks of us is this: that we use our gifts wisely and extend our blessings to others.*

---

* *"In the Spirit" by Susan L. Taylor in* Essence, *June 2003. Used with permission from* Essence *magazine.*

Smashing the Façade

I became more and more anxious and I wasn't sure why. I wanted to jump out of my skin. I could have easily started drinking heavily to calm my nerves. I began to feel like I wanted to run away. Fortunately, I had sense enough to realize that these feelings were not a normal response to anything in my life.

I began visiting different churches looking for help. At a Methodist church I visited, they advertised counseling sessions for women. I signed up. The counselor there helped me to make the connection between the feelings I was having and the sexual abuse. It seems obvious in hindsight, but at the time I didn't understand that having a daughter the same age as I was during the abuse was likely to cause my coping mechanisms to be overwhelmed and break down.

I didn't want to involve Grant in therapy at this point because he was less than a year away from finishing a seven-year process of earning tenure at Scripps Institute of Oceanography at UCSD. The last thing I wanted to do was ruin his career with my mental issues. In retrospect, from a healthier place, I see how strange it was that I tried to handle it mostly by myself.

The counselor asked for details about what had happened to me. When did it start? When did it end, and why? At the time I had no idea. All I had were a few confused and sketchy images from a child's point of view: Paul hovering naked over me with the pink curtains in my bedroom billowing behind him. I remembered a few specific sexual acts. But how many years? How it ended? I had no idea.

She told me I needed to visit a hypnotist to retrieve the memories so that I could heal. Then, the memories were from the point of view of a toddler who had no words to describe them. They were a jumble of suppressed feelings that my brain was trying to protect me from feeling by numbing myself.

She helped me to understand that in order to avoid this pain, I was avoiding most of my feelings about everything. Emotionally, I withdrew from relationships that triggered the pain of my childhood. Unless I faced the bad memories and removed their power over me, I could never hope to be a loving, emotionally-present mother and wife. I would never be close to my mother or sister, either. Inability to connect in relationships is a classic symptom of childhood sexual abuse. I probably didn't turn to Grant in my crisis because I wasn't really connected with him on an emotional level. I wasn't really capable of it.

Being numb and disconnected may have helped me to achieve more. I left home at a young age without looking back, moved countless times to places where I knew no one, and suffered through cold weather and injuries. Numbness made it easier. But numbness is less suited to building a marriage, a family, and genuine relationships with other people.

Hypnosis helped me remember what happened, but it was still as though it had happened to someone else. The next step would mean going much deeper.

After the church counselor and the hypnotist, I was sent to a therapist who specialized in Post Traumatic Stress Disorder. My sister, who had been through a lot of therapy already, went with me while she was on a visit from Michigan. For most of the hour, my sister talked non-stop, telling her about our childhood while I sat in frozen silence.

At the end, the therapist worked with each of us one-on-one. She held my sister's hand and asked her questions about what next steps she was comfortable taking. The therapist listened to her answers while feeling her pulse and muscle tension. Then she turned to me, took my hand and began asking the same questions. After several moments, tears began to stream down the face of the therapist.

"I have never felt anyone so disconnected from their body before," she said. I was a whole lot sicker than I had been willing to admit. The super achiever was perhaps the sickest of all.

Through this kind, angelic therapist I began a form of information processing therapy called Eye Movement Desensitization and Reprocessing (EMDR).

I had to visualize a certain traumatic memory—like the first time Paul assaulted me—over and over again, going deeper and deeper to bring up the buried feelings. Through repetition my memories were reprocessed from the perspective of a child to an adult. As a child, I had been completely alone, without any words to describe or compre-hend what was happening to me. I had to look unflinchingly as an adult to find a new truth for myself.

The first few times, he just walked into my bedroom, roughly pulled off my clothes, and put his face between my legs without saying a word. I struggled, howled, and fought back out of confusion and fear. Too small to win, eventually I gave up. I was two years old.

Going to therapy created a double life. I had the normal life of a working mom: cooking, shopping, day care drop-off, office work, phone calls, and meetings with my part-time employees. Then, once a week I would spend an hour as a helpless child, re-experiencing years of abuse. With years of memories to reprocess, it was a long, painful process.

As my stepfather's attacks continued regularly, I became totally passive with utter despair. Fighting was useless and help would never come. I felt worthless and abandoned, even by God. I was like his rag doll. He could rub himself on me, play with me, nothing mattered anymore.

I was afraid to tell my mother what was happening because it might upset her and break up our family. I had already lost one father. I didn't know I had any other choice except keeping the family together and obeying my father. When it is your own home, there is nowhere to go to escape.

I felt trapped and utterly without hope. Childhood usually is a time of the carefree joy, but at age two I was passive and joyless. In therapy, as I relived my toddler years, I could feel only emptiness, a bleak wasteland stretching before me. I wanted nothing, cared about nothing.

Badly shaken after each hour of therapy, I stopped for a cup of coffee and a chocolate chip cookie to pull myself together enough to pick up my daughter from day care and ask about her day.

Johnnetta B. Cole

Johnnetta B. Cole was president of Spelman College, the leading historically-black women's college, from 1987 to 1997. She devoted her life to developing young black women's strength, self-esteem, and desire to contribute to the world around them. She spent the majority of her days on the road raising money for the college. She became a beacon of hope for women, for blacks, and especially for black women.

One night, the phone in Johnnetta's home rang just before dinner. On the other end of the line was a woman with a story she had a hard time comprehending. The woman told her that Johnnetta's husband had carried out a gender-related abuse.

Johnnetta was shocked. Even though it was not her natural practice, at that moment she fell to her knees. Her husband's betrayal went against everything she personally stood for, had spoken about in public, and had worked against throughout her professional life as a strong advocate for the rights of women and girls. It hurt her on every level. It was clearly the deepest crisis of her life.

Johnnetta constantly prayed for strength. "I was constantly praying for the wisdom to know what I should do about my marriage. But I also remember asking for specific things. I remember praying that this whole incident would not become a public nightmare for everybody. But it did. I mean it really hit the news," she recalls.

When her husband went for his hearing, she prayed specifically that the judge would not put him in jail. "It's important for me to say this," Johnnetta explains, "because I don't want to come out in this sounding like I am perfect. I fell into that temptation to plead with God."

Her husband served ten days in jail and got ten years of probation. He and Johnnetta prayed together, they shared the situation with a minister, and they prayed with him.

She says she is sure it is the time in her life when she prayed the most intensely.

Some folk would just say prayer brought them through a situation like this, but that's not how I see the world. Because again, I think for prayer to be effective it requires urgency and it requires engagement of self and others. Without in any way minimizing the role of prayer, I believe I was brought through by prayer, the extraordinary support of my sons, and the amazing support of friends.

The situation with my ex-husband was among the most difficult I have ever faced. It was just so, so horrible, so wrenching, so disgusting. What I remember most of all was returning to a physical stance, going back into the way I was taught to pray by my body . . . on my knees.

Many, many times during that period I found myself back on my knees, just like in my childhood. I grew up in a very strong African Methodist Episcopal, black Southern family. You prayed on your knees. Every night, my sister and I would get on the sides of our beds, and we put our hands together: "Now I lay me down to sleep. I pray the Lord my soul to keep. If I should die before I wake, I pray the Lord my soul to take."

Because of the circumstances, I prayed as honestly as I could for each and every life that had been touched, affected, and possibly ruined. I had to pray for my husband. I also had to pray for the other person involved.

I prayed a lot for my sons and what they would experience as a result of what had been done. It became very public in the papers. I prayed a lot for my granddaughter. I prayed for myself, for the strength to get through it.

And that's a piece that I think is so important. So many people have times in their lives where they don't have the strength to do what's in front of them. My experience is that I pray and I get the strength that I need to keep going.

The way I see it, people pray in two ways. You can pray: "Give me strength." Sometimes I've asked for *courage* or *insight.* That's important. Strength isn't just the physical ability to bear it and to get through it. I also ask for the wisdom to know what to do.

The other way that people pray is in terms of specifics. That kind of prayer I find either not helpful, or actually negative. For example, "Oh Lord, please send me a man and I want him to be this tall, and I want him to have this much money and marry me tomorrow." Or, "I'm praying that You'll let me pass my biology exam."

I tend to pray for strength, not specifics. And the reason is captured in one of those expressions from my childhood: "The Lord will help those who help themselves."

So I don't see prayer as a mechanism for guaranteeing you'll get something directly—do not pass go—from God. It requires the one who prays to also take action.

There's a Bible verse I love, James 2:17: "Faith by itself, if it is not accompanied by action, is dead (NIV)." A layperson's version of it would be "Faith without action is dead." I really believe that. Am I just going to pray to God that it's going to happen and do nothing else? Oh no, no, no!

It took me time to learn that. As a child I had an obsession with chocolate ice cream. That was like, well . . . I loved chocolate ice cream like the devil loves sin. Everybody would look to see the first star, and when you spotted it, you would say, "Star light, star bright, first star I see tonight, I wish I may, I wish I might, have the wish I wish tonight." Every night, I wished for an ice cream cone tomorrow: chocolate! That was probably an indication of how fundamentally happy I was as a kid.

Going back to those two ways that people pray, asking for specific things is more a wish than a prayer.

Prayer, for me, really is about a partnership. Learning to be in partnership with God isn't easy. And I don't want to sound self-righteous either. There is always the temptation to pray for specific things. In the pain of my divorce, I remember that I got into the praying for specific things.

When I pray now, I tend to pray when I awaken in the morning or when I go to bed at night. It isn't a strict routine. I tend to have this conversation with God at some point in the day. Sometimes I am driving from one place to another. Sometimes, it's on the treadmill. But it would be rare for me to go twenty-four hours without putting myself into that conversation.

In the morning, I awaken at five o'clock, lie in bed and am just still. If I have a particularly challenging day ahead of me, I'll use the morning before I get up or perhaps the night before, to center myself, to seek the calm and the wisdom I need.

I don't say: "I have a faculty meeting today. Oh Lord, please don't let that faculty come after me. Let's just keep them quiet." It's more like: "I need wisdom. I need to remain professional, rational, and patient."

It's more effective for me to pray for God to work on me than it is for me to pray for God to work on all the other people around me. That's what I mean by defining prayer as activation of my partnership with God. Other people, they gotta get their own partnership! I'm in the position to try to take care of mine. They gotta get their own partnership!

I usually pray about five to ten minutes. I think lengthy prayers are less important than building a consistent relationship over time. It's the ongoing conversation that matters.

I do go to church, when I can. And I really have to say when I can, because, unfortunately, my weeks do not end on Friday. When I came out of retirement in 2002 to head up Bennett College, the only other black women's institution in the US, my schedule went crazy again. I am trying to remember a Sunday recently when I've been home.

I often lead others in formal prayer as well. I often preside over students in chapel at Bennett. Bennett College for Women is a United Methodist Church-related school. Before we begin a board meeting, we pray. Before individual committee meetings, we pray.

I certainly have prayed about things in my professional life. The most recent would be: "Lord, please help me to know, help me figure out, should I go to Bennett College?" That was a huge decision.

To come out of retirement to go to a place that was in such a challenged position was a big decision. Bennett had a $3.8 million deficit, enrollment was plummeting, and the maintenance of the buildings and grounds had been very deferred. So getting it back on track would require a lot more than 3.8 million dollars.

In addition, the accrediting agency, the Southern Association of Colleges and Schools, had Bennett on probation for fiscal instability, although not for academic problems. If we had not been removed from probation, the next stage would've been to lose accreditation. And when you lose accreditation, your students can no longer receive financial aid. That would've closed the doors.

I was essentially being asked to come out of retirement to take on a school that was one step away from closing down. It meant changing everything for me. It meant moving. It meant going back into a full-time job. It was not an attractive proposition.

There were two very high profile individuals that were so instrumental in that decision. I don't want to be disrespectful or take these things lightly and say that *God sent them*. But I kept praying for the wisdom to make the right decision and these two individuals were very key.

The first person was Maya Angelou, who asked me to come to her home in Winston-Salem, North Carolina. She knew of what had happened with my divorce and she called me up.

She said, "Come, let me help you heal. It's gonna be a long process, but let me contribute to it."

Who could refuse this offer? "We'll have a good week-end," Dr. Angelou explained. "Just the two of us. We'll cook some special things. We'll read some poetry."

I thought to myself, "Awwww, she's gonna put it to me!"

She put it to me, all right! She looked me in the eye with, deep, deep, deep sincerity and said, "You know, Johnnetta, I truly believe that God is calling you to go to Bennett."

Maya Angelou was very influential in my decision to go to Bennett. She told me that in every and any way she could, she would be supportive. At the end of that weekend we spent together, I had a very clear message. Unequivocally, I felt the responsibility to go to Bennett. But still I struggled.

I kept praying, "God, I know this is what I am supposed to do, but I don't yet know if this is what I want to do." At that time I remember thinking that I should call up Bill Cosby, and I did. He formulated a question that was just the perfect question. He said, "Well, I am going to tell ya'. If you're going to be the one to do this, if this isn't going to bring you some joy, you betta' leave it alone."

This is a good example of what I mean about prayer. Instead of praying: "Lord, make the decision," I prefer to pray, "Give me the ability to frame the questions so that the best decision can be made." Dr. Bill helped me cross that line.

I never doubted my decision. Even when I am so physically exhausted, I know it was the right decision. I know it wasn't a mistake, not only because I've been able to work with others to help turn the corner for Bennett, but also because I myself have healed so well. I was taught that when one door is locked or closed, God is about to open another one. I also was taught the Lord never puts on you more than you can bear.

The alumni came forward my first year as president of Bennett and raised over $1 million, while doubling alumni participation from fourteen percent giving to thirty percent giving. We have increased our endowment from seven to ten million dollars. Our campus is looking mighty good! I feel so absolutely and positively good about saving a college that serves many black women who might not get the support to complete an education elsewhere.

It has also been helpful for me to heal from my divorce. Yes, I am helping Bennett, but Bennett has also helped me.

I have healed to the extent that I am in a very special relationship now. I am engaged to J.D., a wonderful man. One of a zillion special things about J.D., one of the many, many things that I treasure about him, is the way that he prays. Sometimes we pray together. It's not a long, let-us-get-down-on-our-knees-and-pray, but each of us treasures this relationship and each of us continues to seek guidance, strength, wisdom, insight.

A Cry for Help

One of my first big, international speeches was for Colonial Life Insurance Company in Trinidad. I looked forward to steel drums, drinks with paper umbrellas, and Caribbean food. I arranged to stay there for an extra day just to enjoy myself. I figured it was just what I needed, with all the turmoil going on inside me.

I received a standing ovation for my speech, was invited to dinner at the CEO's house, and appeared on local TV talk shows, on radio, and in the newspaper. By the time I left I was a celebrity in Trinidad.

But underneath the hooplah, I was still consumed with pain. When the bellman first dropped me and my luggage in the room at the Hilton in Port-au-Spain, the façade I worked so hard to keep in place every day came crashing down. I fell across the bed and sobbed until I couldn't cry anymore. But the anguish wouldn't stop. It hurt so much I couldn't move. When the tears dried, I lay there face up, still hurting with a crusty face. I felt as though a weight held me down on the bed and I couldn't get up.

I was used to being strong enough for anything. This wasn't the first time I cried in a hotel room. Traveling for motivational speeches was my primary emotional outlet. At home, I struggled to remain the perfect wife and mother, stuffing my own feelings down. Alone in a city far from home, often I cried for hours, then put on makeup and went on stage to inspire others.

But this time was different. I was truly surprised to find that I could not get up off the bed. I had never felt so much agony in my life. I felt it would never end. I wasn't strong enough this time.

I prayed with desperation from a deeper place inside myself than I had ever felt before: "Help me, God."

"Help," is all I could say. This was no flowery prayer. It was a cry from deep inside my soul. I felt as though I was drowning in a sea of heartache and might never get air again.

Immediately, miraculously, the pain lifted. I sat up. I looked around. I was amazed. This was the most powerful prayer experience I ever had. I had been meditating and praying to prepare for speeches, but I really had not prayed for help in my private life. In retrospect, that seems so strange. I didn't understand that God, through prayer, could help me with my emotional life. But when I finally reached for God in desperation, God gave me strength far beyond my own.

Suddenly, God was real. I understood prayer was not a wish, but rather something that made all the difference in my life right then and there.

When I got off that bed, I was not the same person. For

all of my adult life up to this point, I had relied on my own intelligence and my own efforts. Strength was knowledge or hard work. Help, in my mind, came from an expert like a lawyer or a therapist. For the first time, I learned that there was a greater power available to help me emotionally. God actually cared about me.

Edie Falco

Edie Falco is an accomplished stage actor and was a regular on the popular HBO series, *The Sopranos.* She is the first woman to ever sweep the Golden Globe, Emmy, and SAG awards in one year.

She came to know the power of prayer when she became sober almost fifteen years ago and believes prayer played a big role in stopping her from drinking. She says "Very clearly, I was being guided by something much larger than myself."

During the time when she was drinking a lot, she kept thinking that she really should stop. But Edie couldn't imagine how she was going to do it. Her whole social life and professional life revolved around alcohol. She had no idea logistically how she could stop.

Then, when it was time to stop, it was very simple and beautiful. All the questions disappeared and all the little roadblocks that she had put in the way were just gone. It was just time to stop and it took care of itself.

At the time Edie was dating somebody who also drank a lot. She thought "I can't stop drinking because all we really do together is drink." Stopping felt impossible. The couple was hanging out in the acting world. There's plenty of drinking that goes on there, and Edie was completely caught up in the whirlwind of all of it. She did not have, at the time, the presence of mind to imagine that she could just not drink at these events. It wasn't an option.

Then, one morning she woke up and said to herself "I'm done." She realized that it was time. She wasn't going to drink anymore.

I woke up one morning and that was it. When you spend any time in AA (Alcoholics Anonymous) rooms, you find that it's a very typical story. For a lot of people who are lucky, and I consider myself among them, they get this kind of awakening. I didn't go to AA until after I stopped for a while on my own. It was hard and scary, but then some friends who were in AA took me along. That's how I got involved with it. It was definitely a God thing that stopped me, when I finally did stop.

I feel like I had fewer problems than many people who drink seemed to have. But I have a great deal of alcoholism in my family. I saw what it has done to a great many of my family members. I didn't have to wait until my whole life fell apart, but enough of it had fallen apart for me to be aware of what was going to happen if I kept drinking.

I wasn't raised in any religion *per se*. Neither of my parents are particularly religious. I came upon this "higher power," as they call it in AA. A lot of the touchstones of their teaching are about prayer. It's couched in all different kinds of language to make it palatable to everyone, but it really is about centering yourself and gaining access to that which we all already have—learning how to quiet all the external nonsense and listen to the quietness, which is everything you ever need.

I learned about prayer through AA, but I don't want to say that I totally adhere to those principles, either. For me, it is God, not just a "higher power," but I find myself defensive when it comes to actually using the word "God" because I know a lot of people get turned off.

When I got so much help with a big problem like drinking, I realized I could focus on all my problems this way. Then, my whole life pretty much turned around.

A completely simplistic example would be something like: "What job do I take?" If I have two job offers, I can run myself ragged if I deal with it in an intellectual way. If I really don't know which is better for me, I just leave it alone. I leave it as a question. I just sit quietly, meditate and banish the question from my head. The impulses that I get after that are, for the most part, divine.

You get a sense of knowing, so to speak. It's only through years and years of trial and error that I realized, "Oh! This is how I work." Getting clarity with your inner voice and inner knowing through prayer takes a lot of practice. You have to eliminate the static on the line. It's only in talking about it that I actually realize that this is the way I do stuff. Even now, I'm clarifying for myself that this is how I go through my life.

I don't meditate as much as I used to. I was very diligent about it for years—sitting in the morning quietly. It seems so simple that you're sure you're doing it wrong, when in fact, it really is the simplest thing there is. You quiet the chaos, and then the internal workings that have been given to each of us at birth are able to do their magic, for lack of a better term.

I keep saying that I'm going to start meditating regularly again. But the thing is, as soon as my son Anderson was born, I kept trying to meditate, but then I'd hear him cry. It got crazy. So I stopped and I haven't started again. He's a year and a half. But I do hope to get back to it. I've never had to discipline myself to do anything. I know that when I'm ready to start meditation again, I'll know.

That's been another big part of the way I do my life. For example, I used to keep a journal—for twenty years. Every morning I'd write in it and I never once had to tell myself to do it or beat myself up about missing a day. Then, at a certain point, I realized that I'm not going to write in it anymore. I just stopped and felt done. When it becomes forced, it becomes something else.

For me, prayer really has just helped me accept what there is. You learn in AA that you don't pray for things. That doesn't seem to work. The truth of the matter is, on every front, the things that I have really wanted have turned out to be things that would've not been good for me. I've learned over the years to just stay out of it and these things come out exactly the way they're supposed to. You look back and think "I could not possibly have planned this as beautifully as it turned out." So you learn after a while to just relax into your life and trust that it absolutely will turn out the way it's supposed to. That's what it means to "let go and let God."

The third-step prayer from AA is a touchstone for me:

> God, I offer myself to Thee—to build with me
> and to do with me as Thou wilt. Relieve me of
> the bondage of self, that I may better do Thy will.
> Take away my difficulties, that victory over them

may bear witness to those I would help of Thy
Power, Thy Love, and Thy Way of life. May I do
Thy will always!*

For me, that basically says it all.

In my acting, prayer and God play a role. I truly believe
that the more I act, the more I learn to quiet myself. Once
I've done the work—I've learned the lines, I know what my
character does for a living—once the technical stuff is out of
the way, then I do nothing but completely relax.

My sister has done some skydiving, and I can't understand that. Meanwhile, the idea of going on stage to her is
absolutely horrifying. Then I realized that skydiving and
acting are actually sort of similar. You're about to jump out
of a plane and you're terrified—just like being backstage and
you're terrified. You go out on stage in utter terror just as
you jump out of the plane . . . and then the parachute opens
and you're floating for the rest of the trip.

The parachute feels like my idea of God. As soon as
you're out there on stage with the audience and the play
kicks in . . . then something else takes over, something far
bigger than me.

I adopted my son Anderson on my own, and it has been
an amazing journey. That's another big part of the trust that
I now have in the order of things. When I decided to adopt
my son, on some level it made absolutely no sense. I had
breast cancer a couple of years prior to the adoption and was
just finishing the treatment, when I suddenly knew it was the

---

*AA Services. *Alcoholics Anonymous* Big Book *4th* Edition, *Alcoholics Anonymous
World Services, Inc* © 2002. *The Third Step in AA is: "Made a decision to turn our
will and our lives over to the care of God as we understood Him."*

right time. Even though I was finishing the treatment, I had to have faith that I would be okay—which I am by the way.

I had a lot of doubts—I wondered how long I would live. I never expected to be a single mother. But I just filled out the paperwork to adopt a son. On occasion, I have taken him to church. People really learn by example, I believe. If I live my life from a relaxed, prayerful, and trusting place, then perhaps he'll learn to do the same.

In my life, the way I pray has changed a lot. It used to be: "Please get me through this day," or "Please make this person get out of my life." Now it's just, "Guide me. Show me which way to go and help me behave in the way that suits You best. Make me more like You."

You have to quiet the static, get rid of the alcohol or whatever your crutch is, so that you can hear God in your heart. And then you have to actually do it, follow through on what you hear.

Part of the appeal of *The Sopranos* is that it shows people in all of their colors. My character, Carmela, is a deeply religious woman whose husband kills people for a living. It's very hard to feel just one way about any of the characters on the show, which is pretty much in accordance with real life. They're complicated. They do good things, they do bad things, and they struggle as to which is which. People relate to it because that is more like real life.

It's amazing to me that people will get on TV and talk about all kinds of personal things: money problems, deviant sexual behavior, or family dysfunction. But when you hear someone talk about prayer, the attitude is: "Oh no! Keep that quiet!" If there is any cure for the things going on in the world now, being able to have conversations about prayer is a good start.

Hitting Bottom

BONNIE'S STORY

It was 4:30 a.m., and, once again, I was wide awake. I quietly got out of bed so as not to disturb Grant and put on some jeans and a T-shirt. I walked downstairs and out the front door. I passed two identical townhouses on our street, which was inside a little gated community of condominiums. It was very urban, which meant there were no lawns or flowerbeds. Little bits of landscaping in tiny oases were surrounded by cement sidewalks, buildings and streets. On our corner there was a single tree. I sat under it and looked up to see the sun rise. I prayed.

I was looking for peace. I read the Bible at home and on the road in hotels. I had learned about Jesus in Sunday school, but now I was hungry to understand who He was and what He had to teach me about reaching out to God.

Once Grant had done everything he could do to get tenure at UCSD, I told him more about what was happening to me and how it was affecting our marriage. Although he had been aware I was having problems, "my" problems abruptly turned into "our" problems. We began to go to therapy as a couple, in addition to the individual work I continued to do on my own.

Both of us wanted to save our marriage. We went to additional classes on communication, personal growth and intimacy. Yet, as time went on, the gulf between us grew.

I prayed, like many people do, wanting God to make everything easy for me. To be honest, when I prayed, I felt that this marriage was not God's plan for me, but I didn't want to hear it. I was so proud of being a wife and mother. Getting a divorce would mean losing my sense of who I was. It meant feeling like a failure. I prayed, but I didn't want to listen. In my early morning prayers, I felt God showing me the path, but I felt I was smarter and knew better. I kept trying to make it work. Even though I wasn't always obedient, prayer still helped.

Without prayer, I think I would have had a nervous breakdown or just run away. Prayer gave me the strength to stick with the therapy and to keep moving forward with my life. Some people say that God can replace therapy. It must work for them, but I believe God guided and supported me through the healing process I needed to do. Certain times in my life, angels have arrived in human form to guide and support me. My therapist was one of those angels. I believe her abilities came not just from her schooling, but from God.

As the therapy continued, new and unbearable horrors came to light, worse than anything I had seen before.

As the abuse stretched into months and years, I awakened from my passivity. I decided to survive by locking away my feelings and destroying my capacity for tenderness and trust. I decided to be tough and tackle every challenge in this cruel world.

I became his trained sex slave, eagerly helping him with various sexual acts. By the age of five, I was completely disconnected from my own feelings . . . my joy came from pleasing him. I looked forward to his visits to my bedroom, feeling useful and secretly more grown up.

Remembering how eagerly I helped my stepfather and how much I enjoyed it still floods me with shame. Even though I know I was an innocent child twisted by his perversion, I still feel dirty.

I began to understand that I was programmed as a child to deny my own feelings, to disconnect from my soul and to please my father figure. They say when you don't study history you are doomed to repeat it. I realized I had entered my marriage with no connection to my own feelings and focused on doing what Grant wanted. We appeared to be making decisions as two intelligent adults, but after discussing things, I usually agreed to do what Grant wanted. He was a new father figure for me. For me, being part of a family meant denying and suppressing myself in exchange for security. That was what I was trained to do. And I did it for ten years.

But something in my long dormant core was awakened by my love for Darcy. This was no logical, rational decision to fight for my own life and Darcy's. I felt a powerful love for Darcy and a new love and appreciation for the child I was. My love for Darcy gave me the strength to fight on and on through the excruciating therapy.

Being close to my daughter caused me stress, anxiety, and exhaustion, while I was trying to suppress the memories.

But if I couldn't be close to her, I could not protect her. I wouldn't notice if something was wrong. That's what happened to my mother who, unable to face her demons, was unable to protect my sister and me. Looking at my beautiful, precious daughter, I said ferociously, "It stops here."

Prayer led me closer to God and to the truths in my soul I was afraid to see. That was in direct conflict with the total obedience to my father figure for which I was trained. I had put Grant on a pedestal to the extent that I almost worshipped him. When I wasn't close to God, Grant was my deity.

In the end, though, I believe anything we put above God will be taken away to make room for a relationship with God. God never gives up on trying to reach us throughout our lives. Prayer was breaking down my deeply rooted pattern of sacrificing myself to a man in exchange for "security," a pattern that blocked my relationship to God and stopped me from becoming who I was created to be. I would have to change this pattern before I could hope to have a real relationship with a husband and family.

My ego, however, didn't let go without a fight.

Most of my life I had felt like a man in a woman's body. Men are often expected to live as though they are disconnected from their emotions, women are not. I was good at making logical decisions and functioning well in many situations. I was extremely competent at work, as a wife, and as a mother. I worked hard. I shopped for clothes only when I needed functional items for work or for a special event. And I liked myself that way. I could perform in all my roles at high levels and nothing else mattered to me.

As I began to heal, I reclaimed my soul, my feelings,

and became a (more) whole person. It sounds nice, but it sure felt weird. I was used to being this very male sort of person, but then suddenly started experiencing feminine feelings.

I distinctly remember the first time I tidied up the house before settling down to work on my writing. I did it instinctively, because I didn't feel comfortable in a messy space. Then I sat down to work. All of a sudden, I realized what I had done. Usually, I cleaned up before dinner, or before company, or for some external reason. But I had never, ever before tidied up just for myself. That morning, my feelings mattered to me. But it was very odd—like I was possessed by an alien. After I sat down, realizing what I had done, I looked around as if to say, "Who did that?"

The person who I knew myself to be was being eroded. It was downright scary. When you are looking at really giving up who you have always been, it is terrifying. That person, the person who began the healing, essentially died.

Late one night, after Darcy and Grant were in bed, I sat alone in the living room, slumped in a chair. "God," I said. "I can't do any more than this." I had hit bottom. I knew I needed to move out into my own place, but I just didn't have the strength to do it. Reliving the abuse in therapy sessions was like having the stuffing kicked out of me week after week. I kept working and earning a living. I took care of my daughter. I cooked meals.

"I keep trying to do the right thing," I prayed. "I'm not drinking. I'm not running away. Every day I put one foot in front of the other, no matter how difficult. But God, I don't have any more to give. I can't keep doing this and I am too exhausted to move away. Help me, Lord."

I looked up to the ceiling wondering what God could do. "I guess You'll have to send a couple of angels to carry me away to a place where I can heal. Lord, that's what I need right now."

I had no choice but to let go and let God.

Delilah Rene

Delilah Rene is the beloved, husky-voiced, nationally syndicated, radio-show host who has an audience of seven million listeners. Her nighttime radio show, heard across the country, features romantic music, listener requests, and dedications. Callers often pour out their hearts to her.

As the guest speaker at a prayer breakfast, she stepped up to the podium, eyes bright, blond hair shining in the light, strong, sassy and beautiful. Then she began by talking about a well on a farm that she bought. The well was a hole in the ground covered by a three-foot slab of cement, with a three-inch hole where the hand pump attached. Her kids enjoyed pumping the water and playing in it.

The government had informed her that the well was unsafe and must be covered.

"But it is covered," she told them, "with a three-foot slab of concrete. The kids can't fall down a three-inch hole."

They suggested she hire a crew to break up the cement slab

so that the well could be filled in and made safe. Furthermore, they warned, the water might be unsafe. She was threatened with fines. Her permits for rebuilding the old farmhouse would not be granted. Inspectors were sent out.

Delilah had the water tested and proved it was safe. She filled out forms. She begged and pleaded. Finally, when nothing worked, she threatened to use her fame on the radio to embarrass the politicians. She got her permit.

Then, Delilah's prayer breakfast speech abruptly changed gears. She began talking about a young girl, Doretta, who was pregnant at fourteen, possibly by a member of her own family. She went into the foster care system, and while moving through various homes, became pregnant again and again. Most of those children were taken away and also put into foster homes until the time when Doretta would reach eighteen. Later, when Doretta was an adult, she was living with five of her six children, as well as her boyfriend, who was the father of the two babies in diapers. He beat Doretta and her eight-year-old boy so badly one day that the neighbors called the police. Delilah described the scene found by the cops: crack, empty pizza boxes, and drugged-up parents.

Then Delilah traced the path of Doretta's kids, the second generation in foster care. She detailed a complaint from a girl of nine that she was being raped by the teenage son of her foster mother, a complaint which was not believed and ignored. Months later, after a school program on "inappropriate touch," the same girl reported being raped that very morning and was taken in a police car to a hospital. After the examination confirmed the rape, she was removed from the foster home . . . but her sister was left in the same home with the same teenage boy!

Delilah's story traced three of Doretta's kids through seven foster homes. There were rapes of the boys as well as the girls. One was beaten with a lamp cord. Delilah's account was detailed, including names of social workers, dates of placements, and details of the abuse the children lived with at each stage.

The story about the well had seemed shallow. The foster care story seemed overly graphic and painful for a prayer breakfast.

Then Delilah delivered the punch line: "I adopted three of Doretta's children." Delilah, as a single mom, already with four children of her own, adopted three of these extremely troubled kids from foster care.

Why was the government so concerned with my well? They sent inspectors, charged fines, and had rules and standards. Why couldn't they put that energy into protecting my children? Why do our tax dollars go to pay people to be foster parents who routinely rape, beat, and neglect our children?

My children will never be normal. One of my daughters ran away to look for her mother and we found her selling herself on the street two weeks later. When they come from a world where drugs, prostitution, and abuse are normal, how do I teach them to love, to trust, and to have values?

I pray for everything: healing for my children, on a physical level as well as emotionally. I pray for parking places, wisdom, safe driving, safe flights . . . everything that I need or want, I ask Him for.

I don't have a prayer routine that I follow. I pray when I wake up and I thank God for the day . . . I pray when I drive. I talk to the Lord out loud, as if He is sitting next to me.

I have never prayed kneeling . . . well, not often, anyway. My prayers are an extension of my thoughts. No matter where I am or what I am thinking about, I try to invite God into the conversation going on in my head. I try to praise Him in all situations, even when I am angry or frustrated. If I am stuck in traffic, I thank Him and realize He might be protecting me from an accident up ahead or something. I pray when I am happy more than when I am sad or upset. I pray for listeners who call or write and share a tragedy or sad story.

I'm always busy. I have seven kids. I have a career, I have animals. I run a company. I am busy eighteen hours a day, seven days a week.

I used to believe that if I prayed with faith, God would be like a genie in a bottle and grant my prayer, if it was in keeping with His Word. I prayed for my mom to be healed of cancer. I believed she would be. I expected a miracle. She died.

It took me a long time to realize that God is God and He will do what He knows is best, and that I can pray specifically, but I must trust the outcome to Him, even when it is not what I would want.

I used to try to do formal prayers, I used to pray in tongues and groups and churches. Now my prayers are more a part of my life, like breathing. I look at the mountains and I think "God created all of this simply to bless us? Amazing!"

I try to be a good example for my kids in prayer. My son, Zack, at age seven, has some unique challenges. He has mild autism and ADHD, he is high-strung, often a wild boy. But he "gets God." He gets God in the sense that the moment he hurts or has a bad day or sees someone bleeding or senses any problem, he says, "Mom, ask Jesus to fix this." He turns to the Lord first in every difficult situation. I *love* his wonderful faith!

My kids have always attended church and schools within our church, so they have a wonderful understanding of how prayer changes things. Knowing that God will always, a hundred percent of the time, provide all my needs, gives me the freedom to not worry. I always remember Philippians 4:19: "But my God shall supply all your need according to his riches in glory by Christ Jesus" (KJV). If He promises to take care of all my needs, I need not worry about tomorrow or my future, which allows me to use my time and energy to be loving and creative!

PART VI

AND STILL I RISE . . .

The Healing Valley

I walked along a dusty, dirt road with my five-year-old daughter on our way to church. Just like in my childhood, it was only about six blocks away from home. My beautiful, healthy, confident daughter laughed and talked incessantly as we walked.

I was no longer the little girl who dragged the brace on her leg and suffered from fears and abuse. Nor was I the soulless woman who worked relentlessly to suppress her fears and turned away from God. In Pine Valley, strengthened by prayer, I began to walk tall and face my fears. In the bright sunshine, I breathed in the crisp mountain air and the fresh scent of pine trees all around me.

I had moved forty-five miles inland from the beaches of San Diego to Pine Valley, a town of 1,600 people on the edge of a national forest in the foothills of the Laguna Mountains, at 4,000 feet in altitude.

The town itself was only three blocks long, with no stop

lights and no sidewalks. There was a post office, a library, a volunteer fire station, a sheriff's office, a small grocery store, two restaurants, a video store, and a diner. I loved the simple things, like walking to the post office or sitting in the diner and hearing the news about everyone in town. I worked by phone and e-mail, flying across the country a few times each month to give motivational speeches. It felt like heaven on earth.

Once Darcy and I arrived at the cinder-block community center where our nondenominational Sunday service was held, people greeted us warmly. In such a small town, everyone was a neighbor and our kids all went to school together. Maybe fifty or sixty people came together each Sunday for a service that was not fancy, but some of the most powerful worship times I have ever had.

We had no organ or choir, only a piano player and sometimes a guitar or two. While an impressive church can be a blessing, this was proof that the Spirit can move powerfully even in the humblest of places.

Darcy was attending church regularly for the first time in her life. She accepted Jesus into her heart and began learning about the Bible. Pastor Chuck Hanson and his wife Marge embraced me, prayed with me, and guided me. I had found a church home for the first time since Sunday school.

I had prayed for God to send His angels to lift me up and carry me to where I needed to go. I realized that, indeed, He had. Two women appeared to help me make the transition, a Realtor and a decorator. The Realtor, Valerie York, took me all over San Diego County, covering hundreds of miles, looking not just for a house, but for a healing place, a place I could love. The second woman who appeared to help me was starting a business as a decorator. Coralee Rogers offered a total service in which she would act as a project manager. She hired painters, helped me find furniture, rugs, and every little thing I needed to move in with my daughter. I was so broken down and spiritually exhausted, but God sent angels to carry me forward and give me the courage to continue to heal.

I kept going to therapy.

The most shocking revelation in all my therapy was what happened when my stepfather abruptly stopped his regular visits to my bedroom. You might think I would have been happy and felt free at last. Instead, I became depressed. In third grade, I went from earning As to Cs. I felt I had done something wrong and lost my father's "affection." Remember, since he had started on me at age two, by age seven I had no real memory of life being any other way.

To feel how he could twist a pure and beautiful child—me—into someone who was depressed about *not* being abused angered me more than anything else. Surely hell is a place where a man can take a beautiful, innocent and loving child and turn her into someone who needs and wants to be abused. But heaven is a place where even she can heal.

I know what I've been through isn't unique. When you think of all the people suffering from physical or emotional abuse, alcoholic or drug-addicted families, or other wounds, it probably includes most of us.

Many people who are doing their healing work are regarded as weak or wallowing in the past. But I can tell you now, it took more courage to face the pain and stop the cycle than it did to ski at sixty-five miles per hour on one leg or work in the White House. Healing my wounds was the most courageous thing I have ever done. I could never have gotten through it without prayer.

Kathie Lee Gifford

Born Kathryn Lee Epstein, singer, songwriter, actor, and producer, Kathie Lee Gifford is most famous for her fifteen years on the television talk show *Live with Regis and Kathie Lee,* which she co-hosted with Regis Philbin.

Her fans were shocked when headlines accused her of running sweatshops in different parts of the world. Kathie Lee had licensed her name to a clothing line for Wal-Mart stores. The apparel was produced at a Honduran plant that abused child labor and a New York factory that was said to have cheated workers of their wages.

At the time the news broke, Kathie Lee was just about to open a $7 million home for AIDS and crack babies in New York City, using the proceeds from her clothing line.

She was stunned and devastated by the accusations. She had been a child advocate her entire life. "To be accused of abusing children was devastating," she said. "I can't even describe how excruciating that was."

The worst part for Kathie was that it seemed that people wanted to believe it. A man testified before Congress, accusing her of having sweatshops. Three months later, he publicly apologized to her, but few if any newspapers, magazines, or other media outlets covered that part of the story. She was stunned that someone could stand up and say, "This woman runs sweatshops," and not be held accountable for that accusation.

Kathie says she cried out to the Lord for help. "I really do believe that the will of God never leads you where the grace of God will not keep you," said Kathie Lee. For whatever reason, this had happened and she tried to find the Lord in it.

I went to meet with the late Cardinal John O'Connor, the eleventh bishop of the Roman Catholic Archdiocese of New York. He was so kind to me. After I shared how difficult the last months had been, he tenderly told me something that absolutely changed my life. He said, "Kathie Lee, our Lord did not change this world so much through His miracles as through His suffering. If you are willing to suffer this injustice for His sake, imagine how you can change the world."

His words hit me like a ton of bricks. I realized that I was so focused on my own hurt and despair that I couldn't see that maybe God wanted me to help people by getting involved.

I learned all I could about sweatshops. I went before Congress and testified on a bill to ban the import of goods produced by child labor. My focus on my own pain suddenly seemed very selfish and insignificant to me.

I prayed and prayed, "Lord, if this be Your will, teach me. Lord, if You want me here, You have got to show me why or else I am going to quit. I also bear Your name. I don't want You being dragged into the mud with all of this."

What I needed was to take my eyes off of me and get my eyes back on the Lord and on the real suffering of other people. As bad as I felt going through that time, it was nothing compared to all the anguish and despair of little kids and other people in life who are victims of truly evil people only focused on making a buck at the end of the day. I got a huge education out of that.

I ended up working with Congress and [then] President Clinton and we changed the laws. My president, governor, attorney general, and secretary of labor all literally said to me "You are the only person who is going to be able to change this." They told me that sweatshops have been a problem for hundreds of years, but until my name was in the newspapers and people became aware of it, little had been done. Because of the publicity, landmark legislation was passed.

I don't think I would have had the courage to stand up to this fight if I hadn't known the Lord. The Holy Spirit kicked in and said, "Wait a minute. All things work together for good for those who love God (see Romans 8:28). That means all things—not just that beautiful baby girl you had a couple of years ago—but this crisis as well." That is the hard walk with the Lord; not just the good times, but the tough times, too.

The Bible says to pray without ceasing (see I Thessalonians 5:17). To me, that says our lives are meant to be a prayer. Once I realized that, it changed everything for me. I realized that if I was to truly pray without ceasing, it meant that my life is to be a prayer from the minute I wake up in the morning. I begin the day in prayer—even before I get out of bed—my first thought is on Him.

Once you start realizing that your life is to be a prayer in itself, it just makes each moment so much more precious because you are always in the presence of the Holy One. That impacts how you speak, where you go, and what you spend your time doing. It makes the awareness of your Lord just that much more profound. I don't know that there was one particular moment when I came to understand that. It has just been a process.

I was almost thirteen years old when I came to know the Lord. That's the age my daughter, Cassie, is now. I am so grateful that she and my son, Cody, have known Him as their friend so much earlier than I did. I can't even imagine the lifelong impact that will have on my children. I think the best gift we could ever give our children is the knowledge that we as parents love them, but also that their heavenly Father loves them even more than we do.

People always ask me if it was difficult to be a Christian in show business. I always have the exact same answer. How can I be in show business *without* being a Christian? I don't ask other people how they can be a plumber or a politician and be a Christian.

I have always been uncomfortable with cookie-cutter Christianity. God, in His omnipotence, made every one of us unique. He made me with the kinds of gifts and skills that I have. I can't turn on a computer, but I can turn on an audience. I can't cook very well, but I can cook up controversy. He uses my gifts, if I am willing, for His purposes.

It is so comforting to know that God has a purpose for us until our very last breath, and then even beyond.

Putting Suffering on the Altar

I sat on the floor of a cellar in a big, old house in Baltimore. I was in Baltimore to give a speech for a major corporation, but I had agreed to drop by this shelter for runaway teen girls while I was in town. Their temporary housing was upstairs, but I waited to meet them in this windowless cellar with plain white walls, dark brown carpeting, and no furniture, except a small two-seater couch.

I prayed as I waited for them. I prayed for a way to reach them and connect with their hearts. My degrees from Harvard or Oxford would not impress them or make them feel close to me. Stories about ski racing would sound like stories from outer space to these inner-city, homeless girls. They were struggling with problems like finding the next safe place to eat and sleep. Many of them were probably escaping physical or mental abuse. I searched my heart for something that would be of use to them.

When nine girls shuffled down the stairs to join me

on the floor or sit on the small sofa, I could feel the layers of toughness and cynicism they all wore. They did not look pleased to see me or interested in anything I had to say. They either talked to each other or sat sullenly and ignored me.

I introduced myself, took off my leg and passed it around. They were horrified and fascinated. At least it got their attention.

"I don't know if I could stand that," one girl said. "Not having my leg."

These hardened girls saw that there might be something more difficult than what they were dealing with in their own lives. I earned enough respect from them so that they would listen to what I had to say.

I talked about losing my leg, the pain of learning to walk, and being teased by other kids. Then I shared my history of sexual abuse and the road to healing. At this point some of the girls began telling me their problems. By the end of two hours we were laughing and crying together.

I had pierced their bravado and touched their souls. My prayer was answered. I began to understand that God could use my deepest pain to help others. Like Kathie Lee, I could put my struggles on the altar to serve God.

I shared with them that my human instincts were warped. I needed God to show me how to love. I knew I had to pray and build a close relationship with God to have any hope of knowing love.

As I traveled to conventions to speak, I also spoke to more church groups, women's groups, and disadvantaged youth, sharing my story of healing. Back in Pine Valley, I spent hours sitting on my lawn praying while breathing in the pine trees, feeling the earth, and being supported by the mountains around me.

I found the courage to talk to my mother more about what had happened in the past. It was an important part of what was happening to me and why I was getting a divorce. For her to refuse to hear anything about it was equivalent to refusing to see my existence at all. It wasn't exactly like all the barriers came down and we sang "Kumbaya," but I felt like I stood my ground as my own person. It was an important step in my healing.

At the same time, I felt God telling me that I had more to do than healing myself. I met with my pastor, I prayed, and I talked to friends. It began to be clear that I could not stay in the little valley forever. It had been important to restore my spirit, but God was nudging me to move on. With God's support, I could do so much more to inspire others. Through speaking, I could touch maybe 30,000 or 50,000 people in a year. Through television I could connect with millions. I felt God's purpose for me was to move into television and provide inspiration to people on a bigger scale. Moving to New York City felt right.

I didn't feel like just one more actor trying to make it in New York because I had such a strong sense of purpose. I wasn't interested in taking any role I could get. I wasn't interested in success on TV at any price. I felt that I would do my best to look for opportunities, but that if it wasn't inspirational, I shouldn't do it. In the end, if it was God's plan for me, it would work. So I made the decision to go with a sense of peace.

Another reason to leave the valley was personal loneliness. Having failed at the relationship that meant the most to me in my life, it was difficult to feel confident about trying again. But after eighteen months of solitude, I began to feel the desire to be loved and to believe that God could help me this time to build on the right foundation. I would like to say that I felt at peace about this in the same way I did about my career, but that would not be true. When it came to relationships, I still felt afraid, needy, and unsure.

I rented out my house and moved to a 450-square-foot apartment near Lincoln Center—right in the middle of Manhattan. Rents there were so expensive that I paid more for a dumpy little place with mice in the laundry room and a window looking onto an alley full of pigeons than I received in payment for my big, beautiful, four-bedroom house in the country. Welcome to New York City!

Darcy and I had picked out the apartment together for us to live in and decorated it to be a comfortable place to live and work. Believe it or not, it actually had two bedrooms, although they were so tiny each one only fit my queen bed or her twin bed with no other furniture! The living room fit a two-seater sofa and some bookshelves, with the kitchenette taking up one wall. After the big house, we felt snug and close, like dolls in a miniature world.

We didn't need to worry about New York schools because Grant and I had already begun to home school Darcy in first grade. We relied on a special public school in California that provided us with a teacher who gave us books, checked her work every month, and periodically tested her math and reading skills. When she was with me in New York, Darcy studied while I worked at home or took her school books with us on airplanes and in hotels. We were together twenty-four hours a day, seven days a week, in an intense, close, and loving relationship. Every other month, however, she spent in California with her dad, who also taught her, brought her to work, and took her on his business trips. She even joined his Rotary Club and got her own badge! She thrived on her unusual life of travel adventure and closeness to both parents.

Immaculée Ilibagiza

Immaculée Ilibagiza, author of the best-selling book *Left to Tell**
miraculously survived the Rwandan genocide by spending ninety-
one days huddled with seven other Tutsi women, ages seven to
fifty-five, in a three-foot by four-foot bathroom that was too small
for a sink.

A Hutu minister risked his life to shelter these women from
the vicious and murdering Interahamwe. Existing on just food
scraps and water, and unable to stretch, flush the toilet or take
a shower, the women remained in almost complete silence day
after day, night after night, petrified that they would be discovered and killed.

Through the bathroom's door the women heard radio reports
of massive death and destruction and the inflammatory rhetoric
designed to incite Hutus to massacre their Tutsi neighbors who
had once been their friends. Through the window, Immaculée

---

*Left to Tell *by Immaculée Ilibagiza with Steve Erwin. California: Hay
House, 2006.*

could hear her name being called by the killers as they hunted for her like an animal.

Immaculée battled against despair, overwhelming fear, and doubt. She prayed to God harder than she ever had and fought to keep His image in her mind. Time after time, the house was searched. She could have been found and killed at any moment. Most of all, she feared what they would do to her before she died.

Immaculée decided to pray from the time she awoke until the time she slept, which sometimes meant up to twenty hours a day. She tried to literally pray without ceasing. Clutching the red-and-white rosary beads given to her by her father, the only possession she had left in the world besides the clothes on her back, she prayed the Lord's Prayer. When she reached the part about forgiving those who trespass against us, she thought; "Not them. How can I forgive them?"

In the crowded, damp bathroom, Immaculée heard God say, "Forgive them, for they know not what they do." She began to comprehend that if she couldn't forgive, she couldn't be close to God. She understood that forgiveness was her only escape from the paralyzing fear that had been attacking her mind. But it was so difficult, she couldn't do it alone. She had to ask God to help her forgive. Eventually she began to pray for the murderers.

After that, she felt a profound connection and closeness to God and a promise that she would be safe. Her mind became so clear and free of fear that she began to focus on what she would do after the war. She wanted to work in the United Nations promoting peace. She wanted to share her story. So she asked the pastor hiding them for books that would help her to study English. Not many people could focus on teaching themselves English while cramped in a bathroom in fear for their life. Her peace of mind is proof of the power of prayer.

When Immaculée and her companions emerged from the bathroom, she had dropped more than fifty pounds, and at five feet, eight inches tall, weighed just sixty-five pounds. In the end, more than one million Tutsis were massacred across Rwanda, including her mother, her father and two of her three brothers.

After what she had been through, it is understandable to hope that this was the worst of her story. But unfortunately for Immaculée, leaving the bathroom was just the beginning of the horrors that she would face. The spiritual muscles she built while in hiding would be needed to lead others.

It is hard to pick one story from my experience that I think is the best example of how prayer has moved mountains in my life. There are so many. But the one I am about to tell you certainly stands out as one where I know for sure that it was God that kept me alive.

When the French soldiers, who had been our protectors, received orders to close down the camp where we had taken refuge after we left the bathroom, they said they would move us to a camp run by Tutsi solders. The Rwandese Patriotic Front (RPF) was in the process of setting up a new government and most of the other refugees had already moved to the new camp.

The road to the new camp was jammed with killers, thousands of Hutus, many of them Interahamwe carrying machetes, fleeing the country in fear of RPF reprisal. More than halfway to the camp, the truck came to a sudden stop. The French captain informed us there was fighting ahead and we would have to get out! I couldn't believe what he was saying. I knew if they left us there on the road surrounded by these killers we would be dead within minutes. I prayed,

"Please God. You have brought us this far, now take us the rest of the way."

I could feel the presence of God. I felt like there was a group of angels battling for us, and that they would protect us. I looked straight at one of the Interahamwe and locked eyes with him. I didn't want to look down; not because I was so brave, but because I knew God was there with me.

I prayed for my enemy to go away. I told God, "I know that this person is like me. He's a human being. He has kindness somewhere deep down. I pray that the humanity in him will come out."

I began to see the harshness leave his face. He couldn't continue to face me; he began to look away. It was like he was thinking, "What am I doing? This is a human being. She's looking at me in my eyes and she's not afraid because she realizes that we are the same."

I could actually see evil flying from his spirit. I knew God was there. He dropped his eyes and let go of the machete in his hand and just sat down on the edge of the road.

There were only thirty of us and hundreds of them. But in that moment it was as if the evil had simply been pushed away. I felt it. I don't know what happened or why, but I knew something significant had taken place. I knew that it wasn't my strength, but God's, that helped us.

When we have problems in our lives, it is so easy to believe that negative voice, like the one I struggled against in the bathroom. In my life today, I live in the US with my husband, Bryan, and my beautiful children. You would think that after what I faced in Rwanda nothing could bother me now. However, I cannot pray every minute like I did in that bathroom. So there have been times when I have found it difficult to keep the negative voices at bay.

I was in a job once where I had a very mean person as a boss who hurt my feelings with the things he said and did. Even though it was nothing compared to the violence in Rwanda, I let it get to me. After getting through all those machetes without a scratch, I let this man's words cut me.

Another man who worked for the same boss I did was always happy. I asked him why the boss didn't hurt him when he hurt me. My co-worker took me into a conference room as if to tell me a big secret.

"I pray," he said.

"Well I pray, too," I told him, "but there is something lacking. It isn't the same." My co-worker told me that every morning he read from the Bible, even if only one verse. He would call on the Holy Spirit to guide him and cover the day. He said, "Think about it for two minutes, say your prayers and put your life again in God's hands to protect you."

I felt that I should try this, even though it didn't seem like it would make any difference, since I already knew Christ as my savior and prayed.

After one week, my husband said, "What happened to you? You are different." My husband did not see my new prayer routine because I went into another room to do it. He did not know that I did it, but he felt it. I wasn't leaning on my husband so hard, calling him at work, or looking for so much reassurance. He saw a new confidence in me.

"Tell me what happened," he said. And when I explained, he said, "I want to do the same." So my husband began to pray every morning and evening with me. Even though we both had the same Catholic faith before, now he was focused on prayer in a new way. I felt so blessed to have a husband who really prayed.

I think it's a constant battle to stay connected with God.

You can't just reach out to Him one day in a moment of need and then just expect to go on with your life after the crisis passes. Tomorrow comes and we will be in trouble again. Keeping that connection going every morning and evening, even if it is just for five minutes, is what makes us stronger . . . it is very powerful.

New Prayer Routine

With my new life in New York, I began a new routine of prayer and exercise. Every morning, I woke up, did fifteen minutes of yoga stretches with a CD, prayed for about thirty minutes, and then lifted weights or jumped rope. It took almost two hours to do it all.

The yoga stretches relaxed my mind and awakened my spirit. Sometimes Darcy joined me. After the yoga, I turned to prayer. My sister had given me a book titled *How to Listen to God** that I used as a model to help me focus more on what God had to tell me than the other way around.

I began to pray by sitting still and feeling love and gratitude toward God. I usually asked, "God, what do I need to know today?" Many, many times the answer was simply how much God loved me. Daily doses of being loved by God, and

---

* How to Listen to God: A Guide for Successful Living through the Practice of Two-Way Prayer *by Wally Paton. Tucson: Faith with Works Publishing Company, 2000.*

feeling it built up my spirit and gave me strength to live in my tough new city. My soul had been suppressed for so long. Every day that I took the time to connect with God, I grew.

After my prayer time, I exercised. If Darcy was with me, I got her to exercise with a video or use the treadmills in the basement gym. For me, the exercise became an extension of my prayer because I continued to feel the love of God and to contemplate the awareness prayer created. Jumping rope was one of my regular activities. I took off my leg and jumped a hundred times, then two hundred times and finally four hundred times. After that, I did it all again. Usually, during the set of four hundred I felt like falling down or quitting. Sometimes I did.

One day I prayed for strength when I reached the point of exhaustion. Suddenly, I felt new strength flood into my arms and my leg. I was amazed at the immediate effect of prayer. After that I prayed for strength while jumping rope, lifting weights, or any other exercise. Always I felt the extra strength kick in when I needed it.

Having daily proof of the power of prayer gave me so much confidence in every other part of my life. I actually looked forward to the point where my muscles would fail. I knew God would be there to lift me up and keep me going.

After two years of doing this routine of yoga, prayer, and exercise in the mornings, I burned out. I would lie in bed not wanting to get up because I couldn't face the two hours of spiritual and physical workout. Some days I forced myself to do it anyway. Other days, I procrastinated so long there was not enough time.

Either way, I felt a sense of loss. This prayer routine had been my rock, my connection to God, and I was losing it.

In hindsight, I know God was telling me that rituals are wonderful, but God is not the ritual itself. God is bigger. God is everywhere. As our lives change and grow, we must change and grow in how we pray and connect with God.

So I varied my routine. Sometimes I left out the yoga or the exercise. Sometimes I let the prayer during the exercise be the main prayer. I listened to my spirit rather than forcing myself to do what didn't feel good. Prayer, I learned, should feel good. In hindsight, I see that God had a much bigger plan for me than my solitary prayer routine.

Dorothy Height

Over forty years ago, shortly after the Civil Rights Act of 1964 was passed, Dr. Dorothy Height traveled with two of her white friends to stay at the Sun and Sand Hotel in Jackson, Mississippi. The hotel was the only one that would take them, but did so reluctantly.

After the other women joined Dorothy in her room, smoke suddenly began to pour in from under the door. They soon realized that someone had put newspapers under the door, lit them on fire, and run away.

Someone was literally trying to burn the women out of the hotel. Even with the law just passed, there was still much resistance to moving forward. The women opened the door to huge flames. They were trapped inside and couldn't get out.

Dorothy quickly began to pray that somehow, no matter what happened, they would be able to withstand it. Finally, someone came and put out the fire. Afterward, the women prayed together and thanked God they were safe. Dorothy has spent a lifetime working in the area of civil rights. Today, at ninety-two, she is still a strong woman and presence.

Recently, as part of Oprah's *Living Legends* television special, the likes of Halle Berry, Phylicia Rashad, and Mary J. Blige paid tribute to Dorothy and others who had struggled in the civil rights era to pave the way for success in future generations.

In 2004, President Bush awarded her the Congressional Gold Medal, Congress's highest honor, in recognition of her lifetime of work in the area of civil rights, particularly her efforts on behalf of women. She is considered among the most important figures of the Civil Rights Movement, and worked side-by-side with the Reverend Dr. Martin Luther King, Jr.

The president referred to Dorothy Height as a hero who has "helped to extend the promise of our founding to millions."

She has dedicated her life to bringing people together across races, genders, and religions. Her prayers have truly blessed us all more than we know.

There have been many times in my life when prayer has helped me through a difficult situation, helped me to stand up to people.

While many times I have felt frustrated, I've never felt like just giving up. I have found that when you are certain of your goal and what you're trying to do, and you have a feeling that it is a part of your purpose, you don't give up easily.

When you come up against something like that fire we experienced in Mississippi, it seems you always get courage from someplace; and, of course, I always feel the hand of God. It's prayer that helps you through.

I love The Peace Prayer of St. Francis:

Lord, make me an instrument of Thy peace;
where there is hatred, let me sow love;
where there is injury, pardon;

where there is doubt, faith;
where there is despair, hope;
where there is darkness, light;
and where there is sadness, joy.
Amen.

I don't pray any one prayer every day; morning and night I pray, but what I pray is not always the same. I think praying regularly is the most important thing.

Usually, on rising, I take a few minutes and meditate. I sit and pray quietly to myself. And at night, I pray a very simple prayer. And I also usually pray for my family and for some people I know need me.

There was a time when I was president of the National Council of Negro Women and we were trying to purchase a building on Pennsylvania Avenue for our headquarters. I was often frustrated by people in one direction or the other, and many people didn't want us to have it.

I remember I awoke in the middle of the night thinking about it. And then I prayed about it. The next morning, I had clarity and was ready to move ahead. At least I was ready to face those who were in opposition to us getting the building. I didn't take their opposition personally. It was a matter of doing what was best for our organization and fulfilling a vision. That middle-of-the-night prayer worked many times, in many challenging situations.

Prayer gave me the strength to face opposition from a stronger foundation.

It gave me inner strength . . . and more. In a strange way, I found that people I did not know and corporations I had never dealt with came to my assistance. They made it possible for the organization to move into the building and took the organization to the next level. And they are still supporting us today.

I think prayer helped me clarify the values I stood on. It separated this from being personal. I found that more and more people on all levels were supportive . . . and now they are very proud that they were!

My favorite Bible verse is Micah 6:8, and I try to embody that verse every day. "And what does the LORD require of you? To act justly and to love mercy and to walk humbly with your God" (NIV).

If I could go back in time and give myself some advice about how to pray, I would say that you can waste a lot of time praying for specific things. I would say that praying for courage and strength rather than for a particular thing . . . is the important thing. We have to have enough faith that through prayer we are able to have our reserves rekindled and our vision made a little clearer. That's the best thing to pray for because it may be that the particular thing you had in mind is not really what God meant for you to do.

Broken Glass

BONNIE'S STORY

When Darcy was about eight months old, she somehow managed to knock over a tall drinking glass while I wasn't looking. It shattered into thousands of pieces.

I heard the sound and all my motherly instincts kicked into high gear. Was she cut? Miraculously . . . no. I peeled her shard-covered dress safely away from her skin, leaving her in only a diaper. Then, I picked her up carefully and put her on a couch across the room.

First, I picked up all the big pieces of glass. Next, I used a handheld broom and dustpan to sweep off the top of our dining room table. After that, I vacuumed the small bits of glass off the rug. The glass seemed to have exploded everywhere.

Once I was done, I found a new outfit for Darcy and dressed her in the next room. On the floor I saw a chunk of glass.

"How did that get over here?" I wondered. I picked it up

and threw it away. I decided to vacuum there, too, just in case.

The next day I found another piece of glass behind a curtain. Over the next few days, glass seemed to pop up out of nowhere, in unexpected places. I just kept getting rid of the broken pieces.

That experience is what the healing process feels like to me. Although I did the majority of the work years ago, big pieces of broken stuff still pop up in my life in the strangest places.

One way they can pop up is when I get triggered. You may have heard stories about war veterans who hear a car backfire and they panic as if they are back in the war zone. It feels as if trauma from long ago is happening right now. In that state, a trauma survivor is confused about where they are and what is happening.

The first few times I flew first class in planes I would get triggered without realizing it. There was a high likelihood of being seated next to an older, white male. The rows only have two seats on each side, so it would be just the two of us. As a younger, attractive woman, they often wanted to talk to me. I would give them so much attention, appreciation, and empathy that they would frequently end up pouring out their life story, their problems, and their hopes for the future. By the end, I would feel drained and the man next to me would say, "Wow, thanks! This is the best flight I ever had." It happened over and over.

Since I was programmed as a child to cater to the emotional needs of an older, white male, it took me a long time to realize that I could say no to the man flying in the next seat. I didn't have to give him all my attention, energy, and support. I could focus on the speech I was going to make, read a book, or even sleep if I needed to.

It took quite a while to see that my brain was being triggered. It was as if part of me felt that I was still a child, with no choice but to cater to the other person's needs, as if my life depended on it. What is so frustrating is that in the moment it was happening, I couldn't feel any desire *not* to give all my energy to this stranger. It was as if the self-protective part of my brain was hijacked in the presence of an older, white male.

Someone asked me if my history of abuse still affected my relationships. I just laughed. Boy, have I had some dumb dating experiences in New York!

Being new to the big city, I was swept away with meeting so many men who had accomplished so much. I dated men with Ivy League degrees, financial success, and a list of "who's who" friends. I thought it was wonderful that I met men who wrote books and gave speeches like me.

But, eventually, I realized good resumes do not necessarily make good relationships. I found out that sitting on boards for charities was not the same as really caring about other human beings. In other cases, I just wasn't being treated with love and respect.

One gentleman used to take me for drives out to the country: to a special restaurant, to a charming little town, or just to see a sunset. I loved getting out of the gritty city and listening to his role in many national charities. Eventually, though, I realized we went on drives because he didn't want to be seen with me in the city. He had so many girlfriends that he didn't want us to cross paths!

Another man I dated ended up pushing me to give him

introductions to people I knew for his career advancement. I realized I was being used.

I came to NYC very naïve about people and relationships. I used to think, "Now that I am praying every day and close to God, I won't fall into that trap again!" Then—boom—I would find myself doing it again in a new way. Just because I am praying doesn't mean I don't make big mistakes. Fortunately, God is a patient and forgiving teacher.

"You like sushi?" Allen asked. "There's a great place in our neighborhood called Sushi of Gari. Why don't we go sometime?" We had worked together on a television project and discovered that we lived only four blocks apart.

A week later, as I was getting ready to meet him for an early sushi dinner, I got myself into a tizzy. "Where's my hairbrush? Does this look okay? I can't find my other shoe!"

Darcy, eleven years old, looked at me and asked, "Is this a date?"

I laughed. "I'm not sure," I told her. "We're just friends. But I guess I want it to be a date. I like him."

During dinner at the tiny, but exquisite sushi place, Allen told lots of stories that made me laugh. He was easy to be around.

It was still early when we finished dinner and the fall night was pleasant, so I said, "Let's walk home by the river." He agreed enthusiastically.

It was already dark and the New York City skyline sparkled in reflection on the water. I took off my jacket because the night was so warm.

"Here, I'll carry that for you," he said. So far, everything had been friendly but not romantic. Suddenly, there we were, strolling by the river with him carrying my jacket for me. Perhaps it was a date after all.

We came to a point along the esplanade that jutted out into the river, offering a scenic overlook. We stopped walking, but continued to talk about sailing, skiing, and all of our favorite outdoor sports. It began to rain lightly. He put up his umbrella and we moved closer together underneath it.

There was a lull in the conversation, but a comfortable one. I turned away from the view to look at him. He leaned over and kissed me—not on the lips, but on the edge of the mouth. It was a semi-chaste kiss, not quite on the cheek, not quite on the lips—forming almost a question.

I smiled and answered his question by kissing him lightly on the lips. We both grinned like teenagers. I couldn't believe how nervous I felt.

It was a wonderful feeling. On other dates I'd felt like diving for cover to avoid an incoming missile each time a man leaned in for a good-night kiss. I dived into taxis, elevators, even the bathroom to avoid any further advances.

This time, I didn't want to avoid the kiss. Yet I felt confused and unsure what to do next. I felt giddy and was afraid of saying something stupid.

"It's nice to kiss someone," he said. "I haven't done that in a long time."

"It's nice to *want* to be kissed," I answered.

I reached up to touch his beard. "Do you like beards?" he asked.

"Oh, no!" I said emphatically before thinking about what I was saying. He looked crushed. I realized I had said something stupid.

"Well, I have had it most of my life, but if you don't like it. . . ."

"But I like *your* beard," I hastily interjected, meaning it. I liked him for who he was as an individual. Did I like bearded men in general? No, not at all. But since I liked him, I liked his beard.

He understood exactly what I meant and flushed with pleasure. Better, after all, to be liked for yourself rather than for your beard. He walked me home, holding my hand. I felt like giggling all the way home. I couldn't wait to see him again.

Our schedules were difficult to coordinate since we both had lots of work and social commitments, as well as children. He had two children, ages eleven and five, who he visited every other weekend. We managed a number of lunch dates and dinners over the next months. The more I got to know him, the more I cared about him.

One Sunday evening, Darcy was with a sitter and we went out for dinner. Afterward we decided to watch *The Verdict*, with Paul Newman, on DVD at his place. I was nervous because it was the first time we were alone together at his apartment. As we sat on the sofa watching the movie, he began kissing me. Then, when things began to move beyond kissing, something inside me was triggered. I had a flashback to being with my stepfather, Paul.

I became very uncomfortable and wanted to leave. I tried to pretend everything was fine, but he was too caring to let me pretend.

Inside I felt cold and numb. I felt shut down. I didn't want to talk about it. I just wanted to leave. He was terrified that he had done something wrong.

"No," I assured him, wearing a plastic smile. "It's fine. I just want to go home."

"I can tell it's not fine," he said. He looked into my eyes. He refused to walk away or to ignore my emotions. I looked away. He didn't want to put his arms around me, not knowing what had caused me to snap. He just sat near me, caring about me. As the moments went by, I began to feel better. It had been impossible for me to meet his gaze, but eventually I was able. In his eyes I saw such love that it melted the demons inside me.

In the past I had just ignored my own feelings, even if I had flashbacks. I guess that meant I had to be emotionally numbed any time I was physically intimate. Physical intimacy more than anything else, was likely to trigger my traumatic memories in a serious way. Once again, I was finding big chunks of broken glass. Anesthetizing my spirit and not caring about the flashbacks is what psychologists call "dissociation."

But it was different with Allen. From the very beginning, his feelings for me were so pure and positive, our connection so close and open, that I couldn't stay numb. When the flashback occurred, I felt it. I recoiled in horror and shut down. That wasn't something that had happened to me before.

The next day we talked and I was able to find the words to describe to him what happened. In addition, I let him read the draft of this book so that he could understand what I went through as a child and my steps toward healing.

He read the book in less than twenty-four hours and came back to talk to me again. Two important things happened: He read and understood more about the abuse I had faced *and* he read all the stories about prayer.

"I want prayer and God back in my life," Allen told me. "I grew up in a family with very strong faith," he said. "My father was a businessman, but he went to seminary and became an elder of the church. I used to recite the Twenty-third Psalm with my grandmother. Reading your book made me realize this is what's missing from my life now." Allen looked deep into my eyes, "I want to pray with you. I want to go back to church. I need to make sure my children are getting the foundation I got. I have been away from my spiritual roots for too long."

I was ecstatic. I had hoped that *How Strong Women Pray* would touch the lives of millions of people and inspire them to pray more deeply, but how could I know that the book would inspire the man I was falling in love with to turn to prayer? The book I was writing for others was giving to me most of all.

After he read the rough draft he also became very aware of my challenges with being touched and feeling sacred at the same time. He was willing to be as patient as I needed him to be. We could talk about anything. I wanted to erase the bad feelings I had in my head and replace them with a notion of intimacy being holy.

We wanted to pray together for guidance, but neither of us had any experience in how to pray as a couple. Allen held me close and recited the Twenty-third Psalm in my ear, remembering the way he would recite it with his Grandmother Haines.

At other times, we said the Lord's Prayer together. It took longer before we started to pray in our own words. Although we felt awkward talking to God out loud, we were inspired by the couple-praying described by Vonetta Flowers, Janet Parshall, Amy Grant, and others. Prayer as part of an intimate relationship was new to both of us. We took our first wobbly steps together.

Now that more time has passed, I find myself spontaneously moving into prayer on the phone or in conversation. For example, if Allen tells me what is on his schedule for the day, I may ask God to bless him and keep him close as he faces each challenge. I may ask God to use him to bless others as they work together. Increasingly, it just feels natural to let my heart overflow with my love for Allen and my trust in God's support of us as individuals and as a couple.

Before writing this book, I never imagined what it would be like to have prayer as a part of real closeness between two people. Now I can't imagine loving anyone who I wasn't comfortable praying with.

When I pray with Allen I am sharing my deepest being, my beliefs, and my connection with God. As Janet Parshall said, being known and loved in that way is as intimate as a man and a woman can be.

Barbara and Kathy Ireland

When she was just eighteen, Kathy Ireland went alone to Paris on her first big, international modeling trip. She wrote in her book, *Powerful Inspirations,* about how terribly lonely she was.* She found the fashion world, with people constantly making propositions for sex and drugs, and trying to manipulate her, to be unlike anything she had ever experienced.

To feel safe after finishing her modeling work, Kathy would go straight to her room and lock her door. In her isolation and boredom, she began reading the Bible her mother, Barbara Ireland, had packed in her suitcase.

Reading about Jesus riveted her. Learning of His unconditional love changed her life forever. Kathy often said, "I know if He is with me, who could be against me?"

She was still young, but her relationship with Jesus gave Kathy

---

* Powerful Inspirations: Eight Lessons That Will Change Your Life *by Kathy Ireland and Laura Morton. New York: Random House, 2004. Used with permission from Random House.*

the strength not to compromise her character while she dealt with the sometimes unholy world of modeling.

Kathy hasn't just had a career; she was one of the world's first "supermodels." She was catapulted to superstardom when she appeared on the much-heralded cover of *Sports Illustrated's* 25th-anniversary swimsuit issue in 1989. She has also worked as an actress, appearing on television, in movies, and on stage.

Today, Kathy is CEO of Kathy Ireland Worldwide, whose mission is to "find solutions for families, especially busy moms." The Kathy Ireland brand produces affordable products from clothing to food products to home furnishings. She is also active in various non-profit organizations, is a certified fitness instructor, a health and wellness advocate, and the producer of five internationally best-selling fitness videos. In this chapter, we hear from not only Kathy, but also her mother, Barbara.

Kathy: I got my values from my mother. She is such a great woman of faith, a great inspiration, and a greater prayer warrior. Her faith is really the rock on which my faith is built. In order to understand my story, my mother's story is the place to start.

Barbara: It was the trials and tribulations of trying to raise my own three teenage daughters that drove me closer to God in prayer.

Actually, I was in nursing school, and I was sitting next to this woman who also had three daughters. I didn't know the first thing about praying at that time. We were talking about things going on in our daughters' lives and I asked her how she did it.

She looked up and said simply, "*He helps me.*" I wanted to know more about that; I was curious. She was a pretty incredible woman and I really admired her. She invited me to a prayer meeting at her house. It was such an experience for me to open up in prayer, to be singing, praising God, and learning about the Bible. I thank God for those challenges that I had at that time, because if everything had been going perfectly fine in my life, I probably wouldn't have wanted to get closer to Him and to know Him.

My friend showed me how we could be prayer partners, focusing on praying for our girls together. We decided we would pray for them continually, without ceasing. We made a commitment to pray for six months for fifteen minutes every morning. We reserved the time from 6:00 to 6:15 a.m. to pray for our daughters. She would be at her home and I'd be at my home. I always got down on my knees, because if I lay in bed and prayed I'd fall asleep. The only quiet, private place I had in my house at that time was in the bathroom. So I'd get on my knees in the bathroom and I'd pray. It sounds kind of crazy, but boy, God answered those prayers!

I didn't say "God, please make this daughter a lawyer," or "God, help that one get As in school." It was particularly challenging as a mother because we often want our will to be done when it comes to our daughters. But I realized that the most important thing was that every member of my family know the Lord and walk with Him. That was my prayer.

It was later that God answered my prayers in magnificent ways. I especially needed my faith where Kathy was concerned. Only a year after I began my prayer journey, I had sent Kathy to modeling classes to give her a little poise. Kathy was "discovered" and invited to New York for the summer to work with a modeling agency. I traveled with her from Southern California to New York. And as I headed back to the airport to return home, I just cried and cried, wondering how I was going to leave her in New York City.

During that first summer in New York, Kathy faced room-mates using drugs, but thankfully, she said "No, thanks."

At a photo shoot, she was set up to be taken advantage of by a photographer who claimed they would have to share a bed in a motel because there were no other rooms available. Again, she said, "No, thanks." She made a desperate collect call to one of her new friends in the city, who drove over to get her out of that dangerous situation. This is the power of the Lord.

Kathy: In my career, prayer has not been just a nice thing to do; but rather, it continues to be an important part of my decision-making process. I had to make a decision about whether or not to renew a modeling contract with Anheuser-Busch after the first year.

Anheuser-Busch is a wonderful corporation, and very generous with community groups. They fund a campaign for helping people to stop drinking called "*Know When to Say When.*" Some people would not see anything wrong with the relationship, but it wasn't the right choice for me.

I really wrestled with the decision. I had no other income to fall back on. It seemed to others that I was ruining my financial future. When I prayed about it, deep down inside it didn't sit right with me. I wasn't at peace. That is something my mother taught me. She always says, "God is a God of peace. If you don't feel at peace in your decision, then it isn't God's will."

So that was that. I ask that God's will be done in my life every day. I trust that His will is the answer. I made the decision not to renew the contract at a time when I had no other certain income. My business partners were stunned.

But six weeks after I made the decision to walk away from an enviable contract and a great deal of money, I conceived of and began to build my own company, Kathy Ireland Worldwide. It was the beginning of creating a company that would match my values and focus on supporting busy moms with many good, quality products. It would eventually grow to over a billion dollars in revenues. Had I stayed in the relationship that went against my values, had I not listened to God's voice, I would have blocked the potential for my new venture.

Barbara: When Kathy came back after her first summer of modeling, we didn't know if it would change her. The minute we saw her we knew she was the same old Kathy. It was great! She was never corrupted by the modeling business. And now I see why the Lord got her into that business. She touches so many other lives with her testimony. She has raised money for helping children, lung cancer research, women athletes, and so many other good things, so I know that's what God had in mind for her.

Kathy: I am involved in a lot, but God and family are my priorities. In my business I work to support busy moms of all kinds, whether they work outside the home or not. I think one of the reasons our company has had such success is because I understand, firsthand, how hard it is to juggle everything you care so much about . . . your kids, your husband, your work, and your community.

My days are just crazy. I'm the mother of three, ages three, seven and eleven. But I work hard to put God first. I've come up with a lot of creative solutions to make time for prayer.

I put Scripture verses on Post-its around the house where people will notice them. That way, everyone will have a chance to read them during their hectic day. It creates an opportunity for continuous Bible study. I pray with the kids in the car on the way to school. We talk and I ask them things like "What are you thankful for?" or "Where will you need guidance and wisdom in the day ahead?" I also go to a noontime Bible study once a week at my kids' school with other parents. It's pretty casual. People sometimes bring something to eat. But it's an hour we put aside for really good study.

I also have a surfing Bible study group. Even busy moms gotta get their ya-ya's out! It started with a couple of friends who liked to surf and loved the Lord. But it got off to a slow start because sometimes we would go surfing first if the waves were good, and then we'd cut into our Bible study time. Eventually, we got ourselves—or God got us—focused, and now we've really committed to start Bible study at 9:30 a.m. on Thursday mornings.

There was an instance where I was frustrated with my wonderful husband, Greg. It was this silly little thing and I didn't have the whole picture. It was so trivial that I can't even remember exactly what I was upset about. The point is, I thought I was so right and he was so wrong. If it had been just me in control, I would have punished him or hung it over his head, even though it was a silly little thing. So I prayed and I prayed and I prayed: "God, please give me the words to say because I can't do this on my own. I need the words."

In my own words, it would have come out either mean and accusing, or more subtle and clever, but with a dig. Yes, probably mean and clever with digs is the route I would've gone.

I prayed, "God, help me deliver this message in the way You would want it and I will be the vessel." I surrendered to Him and let Him give me the words. It was amazing! When we talked, the outcome was beautiful. It just changed the whole day. It could have been a really yucky day, and instead, it was a beautiful day.

Barbara: Taking the little things to God can make such a difference in our relationships over the years. My husband and I were married at such a young age. I was not quite eighteen and he was twenty. They told us it wouldn't last. It's been a real journey.

There have been times when it was touch-and-go. But our marriage, despite predictions to the contrary, has lasted, even through three teenage girls, a supermodel, and now, grandchildren.

We recently joined a church couples' group to meet new people. We are the only older couple in the group, and so many of the younger couples turn to us for our experience in getting through the tough times. I love that my husband loves to go. He's the first one in the car and doesn't want to be late.

Kathy: Prayer has shaped both of our lives, and today has an impact across three generations of Ireland woman. My mother learned to lean on prayer when she was a mother with children; I found strength in prayer as a teenager; and now our children are growing up with prayer in their lives and have had a close relationship with God from day one.

Barbara: My own mother passed away last year. We were at church during the service and Kathy's seven-year-old daughter, Lily, was looking at the coffin. Her cousins were around her and they asked, "Is Grandma in there? Is she in there?" Lily calmly looked at them and said, "No, she's not. Her body's there, but she's up with the Lord. She's up in heaven." Lily just knew she is with the Lord now.

I feel so blessed that all of us Ireland women are close with the Lord. Through prayer we are creating a heaven here on earth.

Prayer Across Generations

BONNIE'S STORY

In 1954 in New York City, a fourteen-year-old, African American girl named Ruby was walking home with a friend from school named John after going to a movie. She felt between them the heat of attraction that teenagers feel. She knew he would want to kiss her and to be invited inside her house if he could. And Ruby was so lonesome that she longed to let him put his arms around her.

At age fourteen, she was living all alone in her uncle's house while he was overseas in the military. She had left her mother's house after being beaten and molested by her stepfather and, on another occasion, one of his friends. Although there wasn't always food in her uncle's empty house, living alone was a definite improvement. Still, she was so forlorn, it would be so nice to have a little company, she thought to herself.

Yet, as she neared the empty house, something inside her told her, "No." She knew that she could not let this young boy into the house or let him know that she had no parents and no caring adult to watch over her and protect her. As they reached the front door she told him, "My grandmother is sleeping inside, so I won't be able to let you come in."

Ruby: It was God. I have no doubt about that. God spoke to me in that moment. He guided me and protected me. I was spoken to constantly at that time. Prayer is constant—that's important. You don't just pray, you live it. God was protecting me so I was able to say "No."

At the onset of adolescence, I had all these strong, sexual urges. Now people tell you, "Just say no. Just say no!" But it's not that easy. I was so lonesome.

The reason I was protected was because I had prayed about it on this one particular evening. That night, I was sitting in my room alone, intensely worrying about how Suzy just got pregnant and ruined her life. I was thinking, "I want something better for myself, I want an education, and I want to go to college. If I get pregnant I might not go to college." "Help me!" I prayed in desperation.

The answer to my prayer was that God touched me with love. It was like the kind of religious experiences they describe where you see the light or a visitation.

I felt this overwhelming love. After that, I knew that I didn't need to act on my sexual cravings, instincts, and urges, because God was a greater love, and I was covered. It was a very physical feeling. It gives me goose pimples to think about it now. I was protected from all those influences as a teen.

That's how, early on, I learned that I really could count on God. But I also knew that I had to do the work. It's like the old saying, "Pray as if it all depends on God, and work as if it all depends on you." Prayer is part of a partnership.

It's not "Just say no." It takes a lot to say no. I had gotten the strength somehow from God.

Bonnie: When my mother heard I was writing a book about prayer, she insisted that I interview her. She was adamant about it, which surprised me. My mother and I had never talked about prayer before. I knew she believed in God, but she was always very private about her prayer life, as so many people are. I didn't even know that prayer was all that important to her until I interviewed her and heard the amazing story she told about her teen years.

I was so glad that my mother and I opened the door to talk about prayer. I felt it was one of the special gifts that came from *How Strong Women Pray*. When we talked on the phone after I interviewed her, she would say to me on a regular basis that she was praying for me and praying about whatever challenges I faced. Whereas before she never mentioned prayer, suddenly it became a comfortable thing to talk about in our relationship. That was especially important to me since my mother passed away shortly before this manuscript was finished.

She died on December 30, three days after her sixty-seventh birthday. She had just spent Christmas week with all three of her children for the first time in five years. We gathered at my brother's house in Charlotte, North Carolina—with his wife, his kids, my sister's husband and me.

Since we couldn't all fit in my brother's house, Mom and I stayed in a nearby hotel. So there were quiet times, when my mom and I got to talk—in the morning when we were getting ready or eating breakfast, during the drives to meet up with the family, and in the evenings with a glass of wine before bed.

My mom was a puzzle to many people; even to me, and

probably to herself. One of her favorite quotes was from Walt Whitman's "Song of Myself":

Do I contradict myself?
Very well then I contradict myself,
(I am large, I contain multitudes.)

She grew up in poverty, lived in towns where lynchings took place, yet went on to earn a Ph.D., to succeed as an educator, and to become a high school principal, promoting integration and equality. As an African American, she converted to Judaism, yet never lost her relationship with Jesus. She refused to be categorized.

To most people she seemed tough, strong, and able to give support to everyone else. Over three hundred people came to her memorial service. People told me: "She helped me get my first job."

"She introduced us and we got married—twenty years ago!"

"She was like another mother for me."

She changed hundreds of lives on an individual level, one person at a time.

But there was another side to her that was weak and emotionally fragile. Most people never saw that side. Under the shell of toughness, the frightened little girl being abused in the ghetto was never far away. As her children, we all knew this. She slipped into depression at times, but hid it from "her public" for whom she always kept a smiling face and a joke. In many ways, the closer you were to her, the more you understood that you couldn't really get close.

She survived all these contradictions in her tumultuous

life by stuffing down the pain, forcing herself to smile, and forgetting the tragedies. All through my twenties I knew not to mention anything about me or my sister being abused as children because she couldn't—and wouldn't—talk about it. For many years, she really never understood the details of what happened because she simply refused to talk about it.

But later in life, as we both grew and found healing in our own ways, we were able to make some progress. She read some things that I wrote about the abuse and began to comprehend what had happened from my point of view. In her last week of life, during our long talks, she actually brought up the subject several times.

"I let you down," she said, "by marrying Paul. I am so sorry. I was blind." Another time she said, "I didn't protect you. I'm sorry I wasn't there for you." She was in so much pain as she said it. It was as if she felt everything else she had done for me didn't matter—that she had ruined my life. I wanted her to know that I didn't feel that way.

"Mom, you were as much a victim as April and I were," I told her. "Paul was a pedophile who saw you as a target. You were a single, black woman in her twenties, with no parents, no family looking out for her. He saw you had two little girls and he swooped in with charm and promises to take care of you. He was a predator and we were all the prey."

"I guess you are right," she said. As we talked, it was the first time my mom acknowledged that Paul was a serious pedophile, not just a man who slipped a little. She had finally absorbed the fact that it went on for years. She was finally dealing with the reality of what had happened.

Our conversation didn't seem like such a big deal to me at the time, but when I look back, I see that it was a more brutally honest conversation than we had ever had before. She said she was sorry. And I had a chance to forgive her. When she died, I was glad I had made my peace with her.

Prayer, healing from abuse, and writing *How Strong Women Pray*, not only improved my relationship with my mother, it also deepened my relationship with my daughter. As I mentioned earlier, when I had not healed from my own demons, I couldn't be close to Darcy without bringing up the unresolved pain and wanting to run away.

When Darcy was very young she had very little exposure to God at all. Although Darcy was christened, we rarely went to church or talked about prayer. After I separated from her father when she was five, she and I began to go to church together, but not always regularly. Since Darcy often saw me praying in the morning, sitting quietly for ten to twenty minutes, she knew it was important to me, but we still only talked about it on rare occasions. I knew she wasn't comfortable with her own prayer life, but nothing I said to her seemed to help her learn to pray. I just assumed she would figure it out eventually.

When I began writing *How Strong Women Pray*, I let Darcy listen to some of the interviews. I wanted to help her get comfortable praying.

One night, I decided to try expanding our bedtime prayer routine. At night I always said to her, "Four corners to my bed."*

"Four angels around my head," she replied.

"One to watch," I said.

"Two to pray," she answered.

"And one to keep all fear away!"

Then I hugged and kissed her and tucked her into bed.

---

* *"Four Corners" by Jenny Dent in* A Child's Book of Blessings. *Compiled by Sabrina Dearborn, illustrated by Olwyn Whelan. New York: Barefoot Books, 1999.*

Over the years we have played with this routine. Some-times I would change the words around to tease her and she would protest until I would bless her bedtime correctly. For example I would say, "To keep all *bears* away!" and point at her stuffed bear. She would squeal, "Nooooo!" until I would say the prayer right.

But on this night, instead of playing games, I suggested that we pray for the people we love. Someone I had inter-viewed talked about doing this every night with her children and I thought it was a good place to begin building on our prayer routine.

"God bless Mom and Dad," Darcy began, "and Grandma and Mema and Granddad. . . ." She went through a very long list, including her aunts, uncles, cousins, friends, and almost everyone she knew. I was so proud of her. She has such a loving heart.

Then she asked, "But what about all the other people?" She had a skeptical tone in her voice as if she thought this new prayer idea didn't make sense.

"Who else?" I asked.

"All the other people. Don't we care about the people in other countries? People who don't have food? People who are poor?"

"Yes, of course." I was so proud of her. "Yes, let's pray for them, too."

She blessed them. But she still was skeptical.

"What about the people we haven't thought of? Shouldn't we pray for them?"

I can tell you, she wasn't being cheeky. She is honestly one of the most caring, loving souls you will ever meet. She couldn't get her head around the idea of blessing some people and leaving others behind.

So we prayed and blessed all the people in the world who we know, and then all the people we don't know. "Whew!" I thought. "That should cover it."

"What about the animals?" she asked. We blessed all living things and I escaped before she could think of anyone else to bless.

Several weeks later, I tried something else. After reciting our nightly prayer, I prayed out loud with my own words. I thanked God for our blessings, prayed about Darcy's day to come, and asked Darcy if she wanted to add anything. It wasn't perfect or comprehensive, but it was a model of how I pray. Nowadays, she usually adds something in her own words. Some nights I am too tired to say more than "God bless Darcy." Other nights I am more articulate. We're both learning: that's the way prayer is.

One day, I found Darcy crying for no apparent reason. When I asked her why she was upset, she explained, "I'm so moved by your relationship with God." I could feel her yearning for her own relationship with God. I was surprised by the depth of her emotion and excited that she was at the beginning of her own journey to discover the power of prayer.

Prayer and healing matter because they bring us closer together to experience real love. I discovered prayer stories from my mother that I never knew, and shared them with Darcy. I have been able to talk with her about my prayer life as it changes. Darcy and Grandma talked about prayer to each other before she died. It was the courage to finally have conversations about prayer that made us stronger and closer to God . . . together.

Karen Kim

Crammed together in a cement tunnel only five feet high and three feet wide, the soldiers huddled in the dark of their man-made caves, waiting for a sign that danger had passed.

The attack came late at night, and mortars whistled through the air like sirens. *Wheeeeeeeee . . . boom*!

It was just two days after New York City social worker and US Army Reserve captain, Karen Kim, began to serve in Afghanistan. She was asleep in the tent area with two other new female soldiers. At first, they just froze, not knowing what to do. The explosions were so close by and they were really, really scared. Since they slept with their equipment and gear, they just grabbed it and ran as fast as they could with the other soldiers to the bunkers.

This was the first of many terrifying experiences Karen had while serving in Afghanistan from 2005 to 2006. A captain in the US Army Reserve, she was a social worker by training. In the states, Karen had worked with soldiers, providing counseling, assistance to homeless veterans, and other common support services for many years.

It is hard to imagine this petite woman with bright brown eyes, brown hair, and a big beautiful smile shooting a gun. When she joined the Reserve eleven years ago, Karen never thought in her wildest dreams that her social work would ever involve diving for cover in a war zone. Suddenly she found herself wearing, and sleeping with, an M-16 rifle, a bulletproof flak vest, a helmet, a flashlight and a 9mm handgun. She wore the 9mm in a holster, where she used to carry her purse.

I cried for days when I learned I was going to Afghanistan. I didn't want to go. I wondered, "How am I going to do this? Why me?" I was afraid.

Because I always went out with MPs or soldiers, I didn't usually feel that I would have to defend myself. But I was urged to practice regularly with my guns so I would be ready if attacked. But even in practice my hand shook. Just having the gun out made me nervous. Killing people? I didn't know if I could do it.

But despite my fears I *had* to serve in Afghanistan. Through prayer, I found new depths of strength that I never knew I had. And it was that strength that helped carry me through the horrific experience of war.

My mother died when I was only fifteen, but she laid a pretty strong foundation for the presence of prayer in my life. She used say "More prayer, more power." She had what I call kneeling knees—they were flat from kneeling on the tile floors to pray.

She was sick for all of my childhood. Diagnosed with breast cancer when I was just two years old, she later died from liver cancer. But she was amazing. Prayer kept her alive for so long.

Prayer has always been very important to me, but in Afghanistan I realized that how I prayed had really changed over time. When I was a kid my mother used to make me pray the Lord's Prayer and the Twenty-third Psalm.

Also, I would ask God for things like "I want a bike, please," and "God, can You please give me an A in school?" But then, when it wouldn't come, I would say, "God, I didn't get a bike. But now I want something else." Or, if I got what I'd asked for I'd think, "Great! God gave it to me."

I think those kinds of prayers, asking God for this or that, are typical of most children. But unlike when I was a child, while in Afghanistan I spent a lot of time praying for strength.

For twelve months I pushed myself to the limit. We worked fourteen- or fifteen-hour days, six or seven days a week. It wasn't easy to stay centered. I prayed each day in the morning, throughout the day, and before bed.

I would continually have conversations with God: "It's been a hard day. Help me get through this." I needed a lot of strength . . . prayer relieves your mind.

I think it was the constant connection with God through prayer that helped me stay strong. I had to keep my emotions in check. It was my job to provide emotional support to others so I couldn't afford to lose it.

Supporting the soldiers with their personal lives was just one of my responsibilities. My prayers for strength not only got me through the day, but I also think they helped me guide other soldiers as well.

Maintaining a happy persona, no matter how miserable things got, was important for everyone. Seeing me miserable and unhappy wouldn't help them with their missions. Everybody always asked me, "Why are you so happy?" I told them my positive attitude was one of my contributions to the war effort.

Tensions among soldiers in a war situation can be understandably high. Quarters are often close; and to further complicate matters, the military consists of people from all walks of life, each with various levels of education, and still others with different styles of communication and ways of dealing with stress. With such a wide variety of personalities forced together, under less than ideal circumstances, people often got frustrated with one another.

In this kind of situation, you don't have control over a lot of things. If someone caused me problems, I would sometimes get mean thoughts in my head. I would ask God, "Give me patience." Then, when I was calm, I would pray for Him to help the people who were bothering me. I knew they had their own issues and they probably needed help too.

Also, as part of my duties, I conducted classes, teaching soldiers how to appropriately communicate with family members and colleagues. Many soldiers return home from wars very pumped up, with a lot of aggression. When you go home, turning it off is really hard. I taught a lot of domestic violence classes for both male and female soldiers to prevent problems later.

Many of the soldiers had family issues before the war and those issues drastically intensified when they were deployed. It wasn't uncommon for them to receive a "Dear John" letter from a spouse, girlfriend, or boyfriend. And the result was a soldier who was walking around, carrying a weapon twenty-four hours a day, emotional and upset. It is a remnant of war people don't often consider.

I remember one male soldier who was involved in an ugly divorce. His wife had cleaned out all of the bank accounts and dropped the kids off with Grandma while he was deployed. But he had to finish his mission before he could go home and straighten things out. If I wasn't there for soldiers like that to talk to, how could they do their jobs? We had a lot of guys on their second or third tour. They had no option but to just keep going.

I was proud of being a part of the US effort to stop Osama Bin Laden and reduce the Taliban forces, particularly because, like many Americans, I had lost friends in the 9/11 attacks. Plus, we did so much humanitarian work and tried to make a difference for the people there.

I volunteered to take on extra projects, such as picking up and delivering donations to distribute to local Afghanis. But I didn't report my activities to my family back home.

My fiancé, Sleiman (or Sly for short) wanted me to be safe. I couldn't tell him about the times we would pull over to the side of the road because they saw a bomber scurry away. I didn't want to worry him.

I was in the middle of riots, assaults, and mortar attacks. I went into dangerous pick-up areas and had some scary times on a helicopter, but I worried more about the people at home than myself. That was the hardest part of my time there. I had my mission and I had to do it right; lives were at stake. And then I also had everything that was going on at home. But, I had to keep them separate. I had to give it over to God, focus on my job, and trust that He would protect everyone at home.

I prayed for my family a lot. "God, please don't let anything happen to my father. I don't think I could handle it and do this mission." My father is elderly and has high blood pressure and diabetes. He spends a lot of time caring for my stepmother who has Parkinson's, so he gets worn out. My aunt also had a mild stroke and became very ill while I was away. It was hard to hear that kind of news when I was so far away and couldn't do anything to help. I would pray, "Please God—no deaths in the family. Please be with them while I am here." It was so out of my control.

I thought that after working with the homeless in the New York City subways I knew poverty, but Afghanistan was much worse. After years of war and uncertainty, they have no infrastructure. They live in mud houses, there is very little clean water and they don't have schools. The people in Afghanistan have nothing.

The people are so poor that many of the local children have horrendous diaper rash. Their parents would take off their wet, dirty cloth diapers and let them dry without washing them. Putting the diapers back on the child over and over would give them terrible sores. I had to explain how washing the diapers would prevent that.

Many times I just felt emotionally drained. It was heart wrenching to see so many people living in such drastic poverty. I never could have imagined it if I hadn't seen it for myself.

I spent a lot of my time in Afghanistan praying for the local people. When I see people in pain or who have nothing, my heart goes out to them. I prayed, "Give them hope to continue on." I prayed, "God bless them. They have made it this far." Some had walked miles and miles just to get a sweater or a shirt or school supplies. They were so eager and happy to have anything.

With the long days, moments of fear, and being thousands of miles from home, finding connection with God was not always easy for me. Before going to Afghanistan, I went to church activities several times a week because I was part of various prayer, singles, and volunteer groups, and had a strong faith support system.

But in Afghanistan, I felt as if I'd lost my faith structure and community. I was unable to devote the usual amount of time to God. Of course, the paradox for me was that in Afghanistan I needed His strength more than ever.

Prayer was what kept me connected. Everywhere I went, God was there. He was always with me and I talked to Him all of the time. And I prayed all of the time—standing up, laying down—all of the time.

There, instead of church activities three times a week, I could attend church only about three times per month—most Sundays. With help from local laborers, the military built a non-denominational chapel during my tour. It was an awesome structure, especially when compared to the flimsy wooden military dwellings that we lived in. It had big ceiling beams, waxed floors, beautiful windows, and could fit about two hundred people.

But, unlike at home, there were no prayer groups for support. The best I could do was a *Purpose Driven Life** book club with my friend Meredith. We were supposed to do a chapter a day, but all we could manage was a chapter a week.

I really felt cut off from my church activities and community. But the community I did develop was deeply valued and appreciated. Meredith would drag me to church, or *vice versa*. We were so exhausted; sometimes it was hard to go to church. But we knew we had to nurture one another in order to survive.

Being a woman in Afghanistan had its special challenges. Many of the women were shocked to discover that I was a woman in my army clothes. They all wore the full, black Burkas, with only their toes and wrists showing.

---

* *Modeled in the book by Rick Warren*, The Purpose Driven Life. *Grand Rapids, Michigan: Zondervan, 2002.*

The Afghani men, on the other hand, were usually nice to me because I was giving them humanitarian aid. But if I gave them a jacket and they wanted a different one in the pile, sometimes they got upset. Because I am a woman, sometimes they felt they could yell and curse at me, calling me "dirty" and an "infidel." Other times they tried to grope me, grab me, or touch me inappropriately.

One of the greatest ironies of being a woman in Afghanistan was my attempt to plan my wedding while I was stationed there. It was scheduled for less than two months after I got home.

Sly and I planned the wedding and Mass online. He would e-mail me the readings. My being in a war zone definitely put a strain on our relationship. It was hard enough to find time to plan a wedding, keep relatives in check, and deal with making big financial and emotional decisions when we were in the same city. Trying to do it by e-mail and on a weekly ten-minute phone call was really tough!

We rarely argued before my deployment, but the time constraints and distance were difficult for us. At one point, Sly was offered an attractive job in Miami, but he had to ask his prospective employer to wait until he could get to talk to me before making the decision. He didn't know if it would be a week, or even two, before we could connect. When we finally did talk, I felt pressure to agree with the move. I didn't feel like I could say no. He was being so flexible, supporting me over in Afghanistan, so I felt I had to support him with the move from New York to Miami. He wanted to build a better life for us. But the truth is I had been so looking forward to going home—and home was New York.

Having done duty in Afghanistan, I approach life differently today. Now, little things just don't bother me the way they used to. Other people may get upset about how someone is driving on the road, but I don't. We have clothes and we have food, why complain?

I am so blessed that I have God in my life. I have a good family. I appreciate the little things now that I am out of the war zone, like not having to worry about stepping on a land mine on the way to work, or wondering if someone will shoot at me.

I was really saddened by what I saw in Afghanistan. I believe the experience left me with even more compassion for people than I had before. When I saw a homeless man in the subway before, I would get this little tingle. You know what I mean? You feel it. I would pray, "God help him." In Afghanistan, I would pray like that all of the time. I would feel that tingle all of the time. There was so much poverty. I asked God, "Please, take care of them."

When I was a teenager, I prayed, "God, make this person like me." I remember saying Novenas five times a day to find a boyfriend. Now I pray for strength and for the other people in my life. I thank God for everything. For myself, I pray, "Just keep me going." I don't pray for clarification or direction anymore. I feel relaxed and calm about being guided. Now I always begin my prayers by thanking God for everything.

Hungry for a Community of Prayer

Bonnie's Story

Westina Matthews, a Merrill Lynch executive whom I interviewed about prayer, told me she was starting a prayer group for spiritual advisors as part of her seminary training program. Fascinated, I asked more about it. It turned out that I knew two of the ministers in the group.

"What an incredible prayer group!" I said.

"Would you like to come to our next meeting?" Westina asked. "It's at my house."

I was thrilled. "But am I a spiritual advisor?" I asked. "I am not trained like the rest of you."

"You inspire people," Westina said.

I agreed to attend the next meeting at Westina's home. "I would love to have mentors like you all," I shared.

I began writing this book because I wanted to learn how my role models prayed. But it never occurred to me to join a prayer group.

I had always thought of prayer as a personal and isolated

activity. Even when I went to church, I still thought of prayer as something I did alone while sitting in church. In New York, many of my close friends prayed, but we never talked about prayer when we got together.

Karen Kim's story really struck me when she said that only having solitary prayer and church once a week in Afghanistan felt like she had lost all her support. What was normal to me was, for her, like being in a desert.

Apparently, I was doing it the hard way—like what I described in an earlier chapter about being in college and letting my stump get sores all over it rather than asking for help to get across the large campus. I thought I had to do it all by myself. I didn't understand that seeking support in prayer would make me stronger and better as a mother, as a motivator, as a business owner, and as a friend.

I came bustling into my first prayer group meeting, nervous about what to expect. I came in as though entering a New York City networking meeting—ready to shake hands, tell stories, entertain, and make friends. All of my anxious energy, dressing up in a suit, and my insecurity about measuring up to these trained ministers slammed into a void of serenity. When I arrived at Westina's home in Brooklyn, only one other person had arrived. After introducing me, the three of us sat quietly in the living room. No one rushed in to fill the space with words.

Westina had provided some hummus with carrots sticks along with bottled water and crackers. I nibbled to keep myself busy, still uncomfortable with this unfamiliar feeling of peace. Another person arrived. We exchanged a few words without breaking the feeling of calm. Then the four of us moved over to a table in the dining room to begin the meeting.

Westina had prepared a single sheet of paper with a series of Bible quotations on it. She read the first quotation, and then gave us time to pray about it. After an interval that felt right, each person commented on what came up for them emotionally, or in their lives. When someone mentioned a challenge or difficulty they faced, I wondered why no one jumped in with solutions, even though they probably all had good suggestions. Next, another person read a quotation and we did the same exercise again.

When it came to my turn to read a verse, I tried to speak with the same quiet strength they brought to the exercise. This was very different from running a corporate workshop or the fast pace of leading an interactive exercise on television! I was used to keeping things moving at a fast, high-energy pace. I was used to offering quick, glib advice. This soulful, contemplative hour was like an oasis in my go-go-go life. Drinking in the peace of God with friends was an entirely new experience for me.

I attended several more prayer group meetings, each hosted by a different member of the group. When it came around to my turn to host, I was excited and also nervous. Each person who hosted before me led simple and profound exercises in Bible reading or prayer. Each time, our souls were challenged and fed at the same time. What would I be able to offer to a group of trained ministers? I felt like the little drummer boy with no gift for the King.

"Perhaps," I thought, "I could share stories from my interviews for *How Strong Women Pray*." I decided to ask for advice from one or two other members on which stories to use. As I was reaching for the phone, the answer came to me. As soon as I was open, help was there.

When my night arrived, a Monday evening in November, they came to my home after work. I lit candles and laid out sliced fruit, quiche and cookies. Darcy, my daughter, played cello to welcome them. I served hot tea.

I felt so warm and blessed by their presence in my home. After some preliminary conversation, Darcy went to her room to do her homework while we began the exercise I designed for them.

Instead of telling stories, I wanted to allow each person to reflect on their prayer life. First, each person told one story about the power of prayer in his or her life. Each person explained why it was such an important memory.

Next, each person reflected on how their prayers have changed over time. It was wonderful to hear them describe times when prayer felt close and easy, as well as times when praying felt awkward. Even people who devote their lives to God can have times when their relationship with God feels stuck.

After that, each person asked for support in some aspect of their prayer life they would like to change. One person, for example, felt she needed to carve out more time for solitary, peaceful prayer, and not just prayer-on-the-run.

As other people mentioned the challenges in their prayer lives, I restrained myself from jumping in with ideas and solutions. One thing I learned from being with these spiritual advisors was to listen and let people wrestle with their problems without trying to fix them. By standing back and letting the discussion unfold, I learned more from listening to them give advice to one another. Their mentorship helped me to tone down my ego and leave more room for God.

Once we finished, each person prayed for the person on

their right. It felt good! They thanked me for a wonderful meeting. It felt good to have created a special time and space to feed their souls. Meeting with my prayer group monthly strengthened my connection to God in ways that are different from solitary prayer. A group of strong, praying people lifted me up and supported me in being more like the person God created me to be.

When I had my prayer life all bottled up inside, I felt I was running against the wind. Now, in the community of prayer I have built for myself, I have the wind at my back.

Maya Angelou

In 1955, Maya Angelou, who would eventually become a poet, educator, historian, author, actress, playwright, civil rights activist, producer, and director, was in a vocal class with Frederick Wilkerson, reading a passage out loud to the group assembled there. She had been a dancer all her life and would later become famous as the author of *I Know Why the Caged Bird Sings** and the Inaugural Poet for the United States in 1993. But at this point, she was still very young and was taking vocal lessons to enhance her career as a dancer.

Wilkerson called himself a "vocal technician." He worked with Roberta Flack and many famous opera singers. Maya was friends with "Wilkie," and he lived in her house. Once a month, he gathered his students together to read from *Lessons in Truth*** by Emile Cady, a unit study in practical Christianity from the Unity Church.

---

* *Bantam, April 1983.*
** Lessons in Truth *by H. Emile Cady. Unity Books, June 1995.*

She was reading along and came to, "God loves me."

"Read that again," said Wilkie.

"God loves me," she said.

"Read it again," he said to her. And she began to feel really, really tense. She and Wilkie were the only black people there. She was young and he had other students who were serious singers, and they were all white and all older. She felt he was making her look foolish in her own house in front of these sophisticated whites.

He said, "Read it again. Read it again."

Finally she shouted it out defiantly, "GOD . . . LOVES . . . ME!"

I heard Him. In that instant in my life I knew that I was a child of God . . . and knowing it then, I know it all the time, fresh. Just saying it makes me thrill, in the classic sense. I mean, my body—Wheeew!

At that moment, I had to leave the room. I started weeping . . . with the knowledge of it. And I could do it again right now. That which made the seas and mountains, made stars and moons, and goldfish . . . That loves me?!!

It was a freedom . . . a relief . . . a license to try to do all the good in the world. If That loves me, then I can do anything good. You see?

Now I pray all the time. I pray when I'm walking from here over to the chair. I pray at any time . . . when something crosses my mind, I have a prayer. Mostly I'm thankful: Thanking God for God, thanking God for Jesus, and thanking Jesus for Jesus. I am thankful for the idea of love, the idea of forgiveness, and the offering of peace and joy two thousand years ago.

If I could go back to when I was twenty years old and

teach myself something about prayer, I would just tell myself to be more grateful. Be even more grateful.

I know that at twenty I didn't know very much. I knew that I was blessed, but not enough to know that I didn't know very much. I didn't know I knew what I knew. But I am a good student. I do listen. I would like to be more grateful today than I was yesterday.

So now, I don't even say what I'm thankful for, unless something's sticking in my head like some thorns on a rose. I'll think, "Hmm, God did that, too." But generally, I just say, "Thank You. Thank You. Thank You. He maketh me to lie down in green pastures, He restoreth my soul*. Thank You."

I was asked to write a piece, come to the Bush White House, and participate in the lighting of the national Christmas tree. I wrote a piece called "Amazing Peace."** I knew I was taking the idea of peace into the war zone.

I prayed long ago, If the Lord wants somebody nearby, send me. I said that and I can't take it back. So I wrote "Amazing Peace" with a more than passing interest and went to the White House to be with President Bush:

In our joy, we think we hear a whisper.
At first it is too soft. Then only half heard.
We listen carefully as it gathers strength.
We hear a sweetness.
The word is Peace.
It is loud now.
Louder than the explosion of bombs.

---

* *Psalm 23:2.*
** *From* Amazing Peace *by Maya Angelou, copyright © 2005 by Maya Angelou. Used by permission of Random House, Inc.*

We tremble at the sound. We are thrilled by its pres-
ence.
It is what we have hungered for.
Not just the absence of war. But true Peace.
A harmony of spirit, a comfort of courtesies.
Security for our beloveds and their beloveds.

We, Angels and Mortals, Believers and Nonbelievers,
Look heavenward and speak the word aloud.
Peace. We look at each other, then into ourselves,
And we say without shyness or apology or hesitation:

Peace, My Brother.
Peace, My Sister.
Peace, My Soul.

ACKNOWLEDGMENTS

My first acknowledgement goes wholeheartedly to God. It became clear to me in large and small ways as this book was being written that I was participating in a project much bigger than myself. I learned to give God more room to work.

I was truly blessed by the twenty-seven women whose stories are included. Each one of them shapes what this book is with their amazing stories. Not only did they open their hearts, they prayed for me to have wisdom and guidance as I wrote and interviewed. A big thanks also to their staffers who helped me connect despite busy schedules and other obstacles.

In addition to the women included in the book, there were more than thirty others who took the time to let me interview them. Each of those conversations strengthened me, guided me, and blessed me. I wish I could have included every story I heard. You all transformed me.

Another blessing came in the form of Kellie Tabron, the writer who assisted me throughout the project. She created the style in which we presented the interview chapters and researched background information, and she never complained about writing and rewriting. She was willing to help with anything—even researching me and drafting some of my chapters when I balked at the idea. Her passion for prayer and excitement about these women meshed with mine to create something better than I could have done on my own. She is every writer's dream collaborator.

We are all blessed by my editor, Adrienne Ingrum. She pushed me to dig deeper into my own story and use it as the glue for the book. Adrienne's care and persistence raised the book to a much higher level. She is the editor I always dreamed of having . . . an Olympic Coach.

I am very appreciative of everyone I work with at Hachette: Rolf Zettersten, Chris Park, Sarah Sper, Preston Cannon, Lori Quinn, Kelly Leonard, and Jana Burson. From editorial to sales, it is a pleasure to work with such a terrific team.

Of course, I would never have had the opportunity to work with Hachette if not for my agent, Richard Pine. He understood this book idea immediately and got it to the right place. He is always willing to help me be my best in every way. I love his spirit.

Choosing and connecting with the right women to interview was no easy task. I was helped by so many people who care about me and the book: Tony D'Amelio, Christine Farrell, Judy Hilsinger, Russell R. Wassendorf Sr., Roland Betts, Carin Decicco, David Mercer, Wayne Berman, Lorraine Voles, Lisa Caputo, Amy Kopelan, Fred Dorn, Johnnetta Cole, Kathy Ireland, Marilyn McCoo, Amy Grant, Martha Williamson, Portia Hickson, Theresa

Moore, Jim Woodworth, Dee Doe, Steve Rosenblum, Bart Conner, Jamie Balthazar, Ms. Berry, Ms. Casey, Lisa Barr, Amanda McCaslin, Brandi Harkonen, Christine Gardener, Chris King, Michael Kim, Karen Kim, Laura Meija Cruz, Marcie Goldblatt, and many others who helped me to connect with the strong women in this book.

Thank you to everyone in my online Circle of Friends for volunteering yourselves to be interviewed and helping in so many other ways. Your ongoing friendship means so much to me. Sunny Bain, thanks for helping me to schedule and reschedule countless interviews, type drafts, and keep me on track while I disappeared into my writing cave.

A big thanks to my prayer group—David Lewicki, Anne Mallonee, and Westina Matthews—for your spiritual support and for letting me share the story.

Most of all, I thank my family—Darcy Deane, Allen Haines, April St. John, Wayne St. John, Grant Deane, and my mother, Ruby, for letting me write about your lives as a part of my life. I love you all.

Darcy and Allen, you also supported me by reading, editing, listening, praying, and going to cafes with me to write. You have lived this book with me. I couldn't be who I am without you. Your love permeates the book. I love you both . . . to infinity and beyond.

ABOUT THE AUTHOR

Bonnie St. John is one of the nation's leading inspirational speakers and has been featured on the *Today Show*, *Montel Williams*, *CNN*, *Good Morning America*, as well as *People* magazine, the *New York Times*, *Essence*, and many others.

Despite the amputation of her leg at age five, she became a silver and bronze medalist in downhill skiing in the 1984 Paralympics at Innsbruck, Austria, making her the first African-American to win Olympic medals in skiing. She went on to graduate from Harvard University, win the Rhodes Scholarship, and was appointed to the White House National Economic Council.

As the president of her own company, Bonnie now focuses on bringing out the best in others through coaching, motivational speaking for corporations and associations as well as writing books and articles. Her books include: *Succeeding Sane*, *Getting Ahead at Work without Leaving Your Family Behind*, and *Money: Fall Down? Get Up!* Bonnie lives and prays in New York City with her daughter, Darcy.

Please visit her web site, www.bonniestjohn.com, where you can download a copy of a Starbucks Cup with her famous quote about falling down and getting up, join her "Circle of Friends," download a copy of the prayer guide, and many other inspirational online materials.

For more information about this book go to
www.howstrongwomenpray.com